Christmas Market Innsbruck

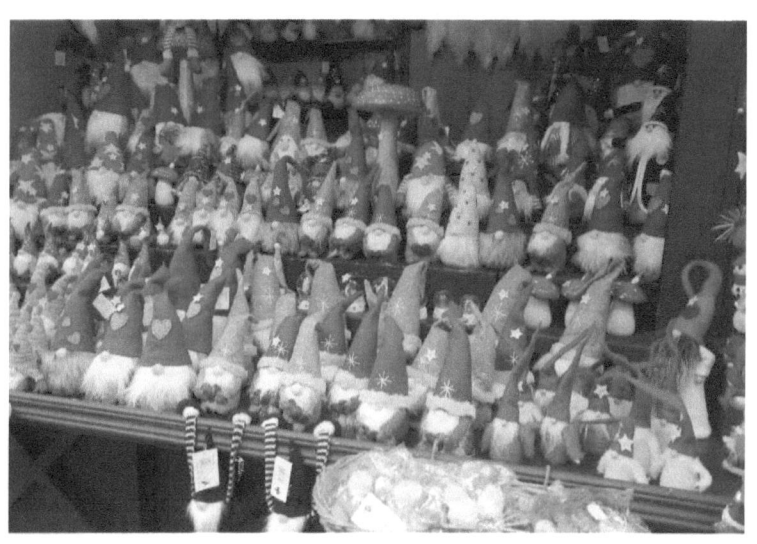

Cristina Berna and Eric Thomsen

2024

Cristina Berna and Eric Thomsen

Christmas Market

Innsbruck

US ISBN 978-0-0060-3363-9

A version of this tittle is available in color print in the United States under ISBN 9781956215816
and in the European Union under ISBN 978-3-757-880-774.

About the authors

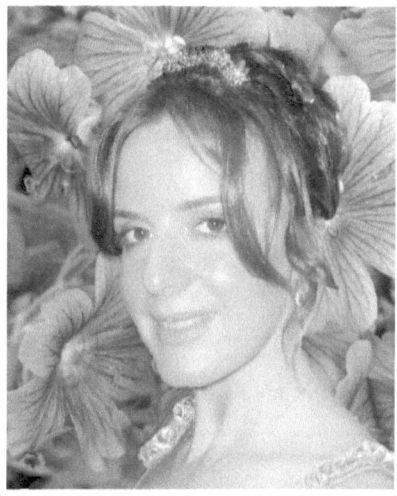

Cristina Berna loves photographing and writing. She also creates designs and advice on fashion and styling.

Eric Thomsen has published in science, economics and law, created exhibitions and arranged concerts.

Also by the authors:

World of Cakes

Luxembourg – a piece of cake

Florida Cakes

Catalan Pastis – Catalonian Cakes

Andalucian Delight

World of Art

Hokusai – 36 Views of Mt Fuji
and many more tiles

Christmas

Christmas Nativity – Spain
and more titles

Outpets

Deer in Dyrehaven – Outpets in Denmark

Florida Outpets

Birds of Play

Missy's Clan

Missy's Clan – The Beginning

Missy's Clan – Christmas

Missy's Clan – Education

Missy's Clan – Kittens

Missy's Clan – Deer Friends

Missy's Clan – Outpets

Missy's Clan – Outpet Birds
and more titles

Vehicles

Copenhagen vehicles – and a trip to Sweden

Construction vehicles picture book

Trains

American Police Cars

American Vintage Firetrucks

Mexican Police Cars

Spanish Police Cars
and more titles

Contact the authors

missysclan@gmail.com

Published by www.missysclan.net

Cover picture: Swarovski Christmas Tree, Christmas market am Marktplatz, Innsbruck, Austria

Inside: Stall at the Christmas Market in Altstadt, Innsbruck, Austria

Content

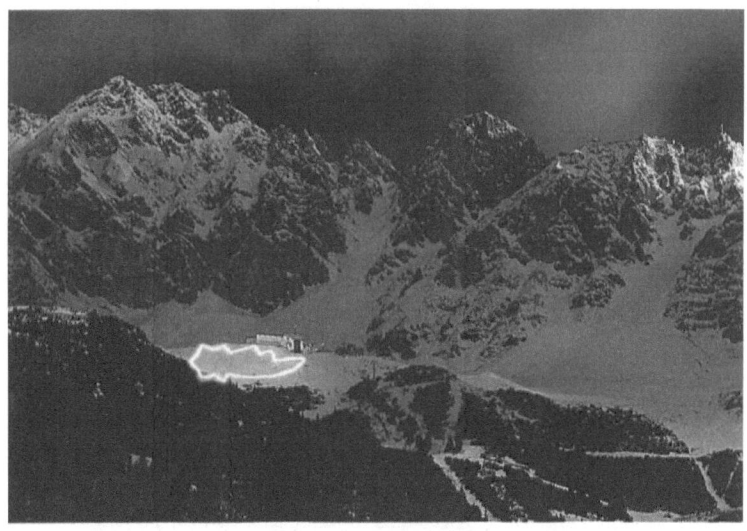

Christkind-Stern Innsbruck Nordpark

Introduction

Europe has many wonderful old traditions, and one of them is the Christmas market.

The December market in Vienna is recorded since 1298, but Innsbruck was actually founded as a market in a field already in 1133 and it could be argued that the December market here would be even older.

The wonderful Tyrolian atmosphere makes this a must for anyone enjoying the Christmas markets.

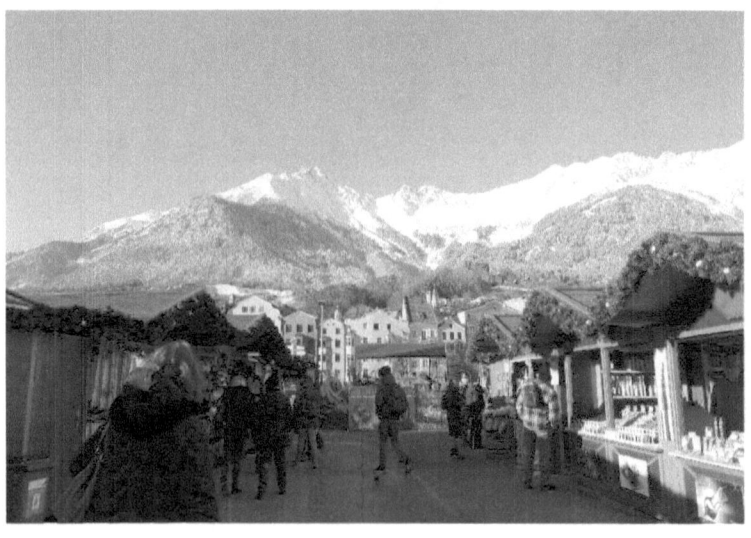

Christmas market, market square, Innsbruck ©Berna 2018

Innsbruck

Innsbruck is the capital of Austria's western state of Tyrol. It is a city in the Alps that's long been a destination for winter sports. It hosted the Olympics several times – 1964 and again in 1976.

It is the fifth largest town in Austria with 133.000 inhabitants. It is a youthful town with a university.

Innsbruck is also known for its Imperial and modern architecture.

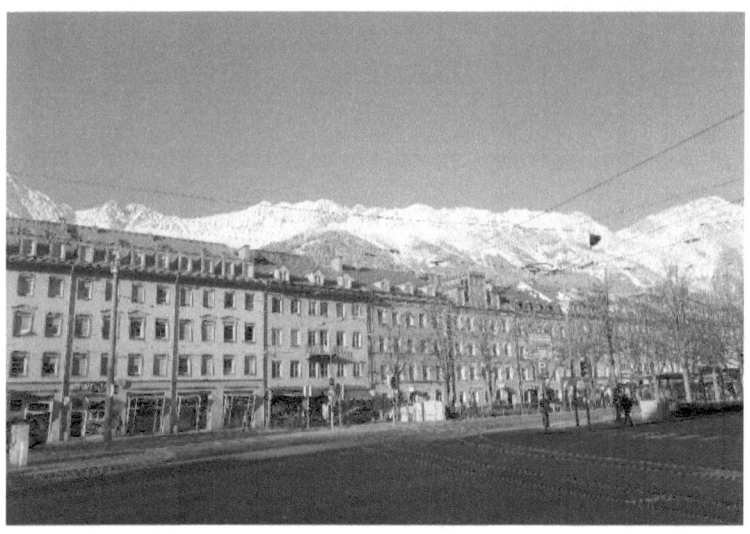

Dec 2018 Herzog-Siegmund-Ufer, Innsbruck ©Berna 2018

The *Nordkette* funicular, with futuristic stations designed by architect Zaha Hadid, climbs up to 2,256m from the city center for skiing in winter and hiking or mountaineering in warmer months.

You see skiers fully equipped in the streets.

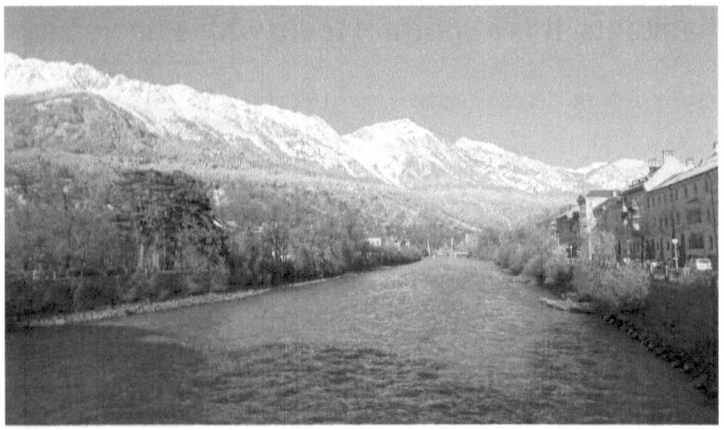

Dec 2018 Inn from *Innbrucke,* Innsbruck. Nordkette mountain range with the ski pistes up behind. ©Berna 2018

The town of Innsbruck has its name because it was here there was a bridge – *bruck* – over the river Inn. Inn springs near St Moritz and confluence with the Danube at Passau on the border to Bavaria in Southern Germany.

The bridge *Innsbrucke* is just past the market square with the main Christmas market.

Innsbruck was an important trading post on the *Brenner pass* route to Italy, some 30 km to the South, the easiest crossing of the Alps. It was part of the *via Imperi* under special protection of the king and the revenues led the city to flourish.

Innsbruck has been populated since the early Stone Age, which lasted 3.4 million years and ended with the metal ages. Copper smelting started in nearby Serbia 7.000 BC.

In 1180 Innsbruck was acquired by the Counts of Andechs, German princes with possessions in Istria and on the Dalmatian seacoast. In 1248 it passed to the Counts of Tyrol, which is an estate in the Habsburg lands.

Habsburg Holy Roman Emperor Maximillian I - 22 March 1459 – 12 January 1519, resided here. He was Holy Roman Emperor from 1508 to his death.

This is the European period of *Renaissance*, from French – rebirth – following the Middle Ages.

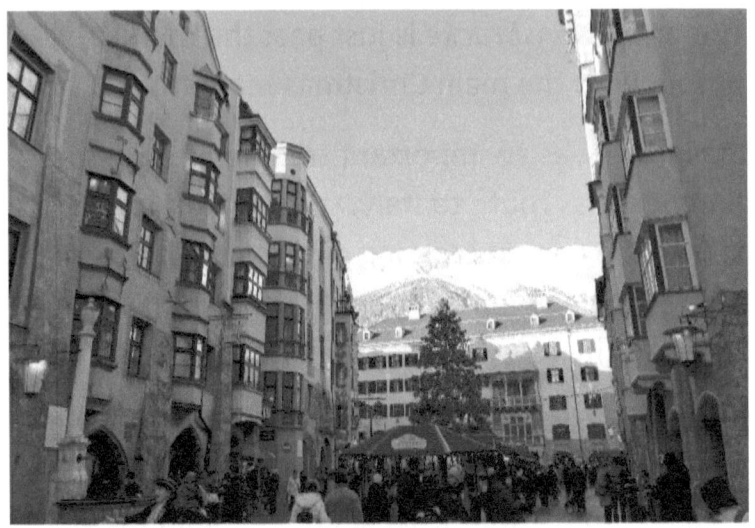

Dec 2018 *Goldener Dachl* , Herzog-Friedrich-Strasse 15, Innsbruck, to the right of the big Christmas tree ©Berna 2018

Maximillian I constructed the *Goldenes Dachl* - the Golden Roof – which is a landmark located in the Old Town of Innsbruck.

It is considered the city's most famous symbol.

It is a roofed balcony, and the roof was decorated with 2,657 fire-gilded copper tiles.

It was completed in 1500 for Emperor Maximilian I to mark his wedding to Bianca Maria Sforza, 5 April 1472 – 31 December 1510, his second wife.

She was the eldest legitimate daughter of the Duke of Milan.

The Emperor and his wife used the balcony to observe festivals, tournaments, and other events that took place in the square below.

The saying goes he had the roof gilded to show his creditors that he had a lot of security and would be able to repay his loans.

It certainly was a flashy way to store his gold and it was difficult to get up there and steal it.

The most powerful banking families in this period came from Florence, Italy.

They includied the Acciaiuoli, Mozzi, Bardi and Peruzzi families, which established branches in many other parts of Europe. They were also merchants and involved in the cross Alpine trade past Innsbruck.

Probably the most famous Italian bank was the Medici bank, set up by Giovanni di Bicci de' Medici in 1397 and continuing until 1494

Actually, the oldest bank still operating is the *Banca Monte dei Paschi di Siena* in Siena, Italy. It was established in 1472, 20 years before Columbus sailed to America.

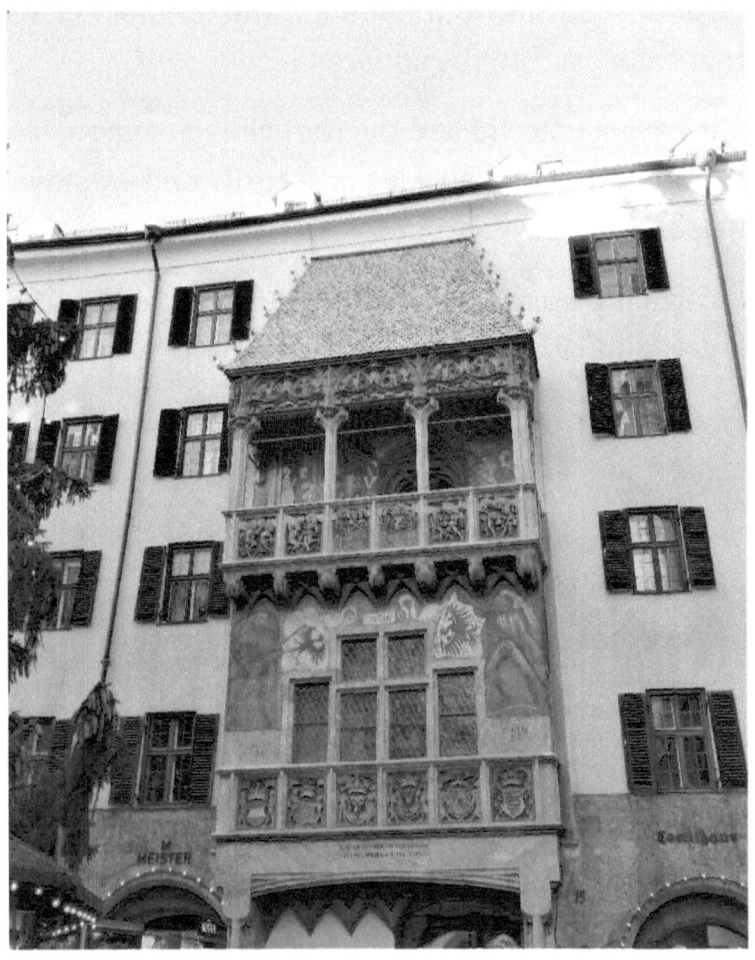

Dec 2018 *Goldener Dach,* Innsbruck , detail ©Berna 2018

Maximillian I was not as usual crowned by the Pope in Rome, but instead in Trent on the other side of Brenner pass, part of Habsburg lands, because the journey to Rome was too risky.

He expanded the influence of the Habsburgs, who by the way came from Switzerland, where there is still a castle – *burg* – by that name.

Maximillian I gained Burgundy and the Netherlands though marriage. He married his son Philippe the Handsome to Joanna of Castille in 1498 and established the Habsburgs on the Spanish throne. His son wanted to be king of Castille and was killed by his father in law, Ferdinand II of Aragon, to avert a civil war.

However, Maximillian I lost the Austrian territories of what is today Switzerland, to the Swiss Confederacy in the Battle of Dornach 22 July 1499 and by a peace treaty signed in Basel 22 September 1499 the Swiss Confederacy obtained independence from the Holy Roman Empire.

Maximillian I lived in Innsbruck which was the capital. Ferdinand I moved to Vienna in 1556, but before Prague had been capital of the Holy Roman

Empire since the Luxembourg emperors, see the book *Luxembourg – A Piece of Cake*.

Ferdinand I was the younger son of Philippe the Handsome and Joanna of Castille and born in Alcala de Henares.

Joanna was daughter of the Catholic kings, Ferdinand and Isabella, who reconquered Granada, the last piece of Spain that was conquered by the Muslims after 711 AD.

The elder brother was Charles V, who fought incessant wars in Germany and paid enormous bribes to the treasonous electors to become Holy Roman Emperor, and he never succeeded, but instead bankrupted the Spanish Empire with all the possessions in Latin America. He abdicated in 1556 and Ferdinand I took the title "Emperor Elect" from 1558. The Spanish Empire, the two Sicilies, the Netherlands and France Comte went to Philip, Charles' son.

Ferdinand I was initially Charles V's representative in Austria and Slovenia, the Habsburg hereditary lands, as Archduke of Austria 1521 – 1563

He ruled as king of Hungary and Bohemia, from 1526 – 1564, elected king conditioned on upholding the Bohemian privileges and in return they pledged to help him fight the Ottoman invasion of Hungary.

Ferdinand was challenged to the Hungarian throne by John Zápolya, a voivode from Transylvania, elected by a diet of lesser nobility in 1526. Ferdinand was short of money and soldiers, but borrowed from the Fugger bankers and got help from his brother Charles. He beat John Zápolya in the Battle of Tarcal September 1527 and again in the Battle of Szina March 1528.

John Zápolya fled to Turkey and appealed to sultan Suleyman the Magnificent and pledged Hungary as a vasal state.

Suleyman besieged Vienna but was famously beaten in 1529 - this is where the story of the *Croissant* comes from – and again in 1532 at Guns. Ferdinand I made peace with the Ottomans and Hungary was split into the Habsburg part and a vasal state of Turkey under John Zápolya.

Although he did not succeed in driving the Muslims from Hungary, Ferdinand was a much better ruler than his brother and more tolerant of various Christian practices.

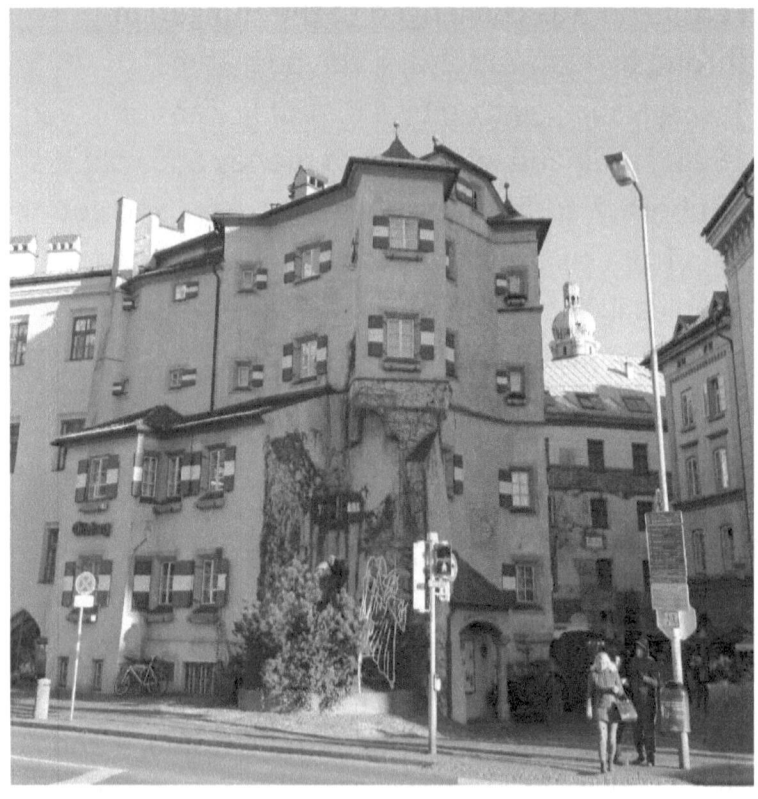

Dec 2018 Corner Innbrucke and Herzog-Otto-Strasse, Innsbruck
©Berna 2018

Christkindl Markt am Marktplatz

Christmas market in the market square, Innsbruck.

In Austria, Vienna's "December market" is considered a forerunner of Christmas markets and dates back to 1298.

Christmas markets became a tradition in German speaking lands and ushered in the four week church festival of *Advent*. In nearby Munich, Germany the Christmas market is first mentioned in 1310.

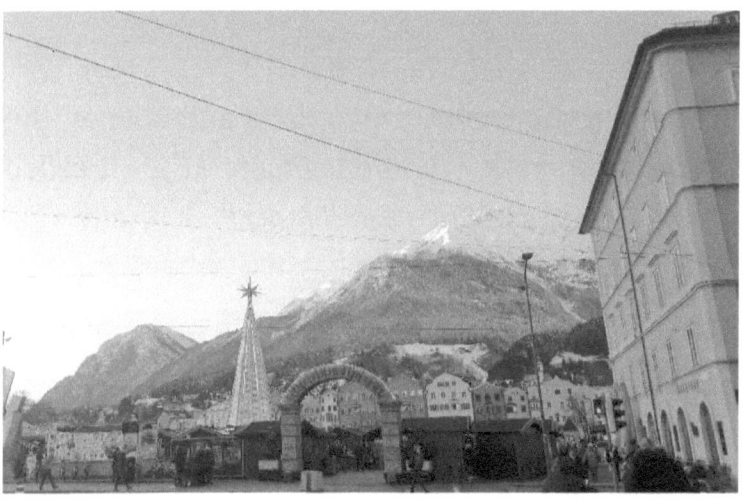

Dec 2018   Swarovski star over the Christmas market in the market square, Innsbruck ©Berna 2018

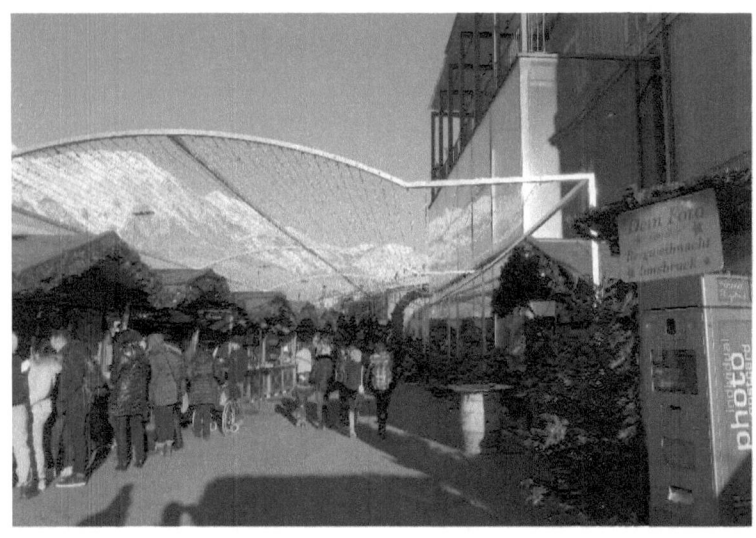

Dec 2018 Christkindl Markt – Christmas market – am Marktplatz - in the market square – Innsbruck. Nordkette mountain range with the ski pistes up behind. ©Berna 2018

In southern Germany, Switzerland and Austria, the Christmas market - *"Weihnachtsmarkt".* - is called a *"Christkind"* or *"Christkindl markt"* - literally meaning *"Christ child market"* in German.

It is traditionally held in the town square and the market has food, drink and seasonal items from open-air stalls accompanied by traditional singing and dancing.

Often the market is opened with singing and a procession of the "Christ kind", which used to be a boy but now is mostly a local girl.

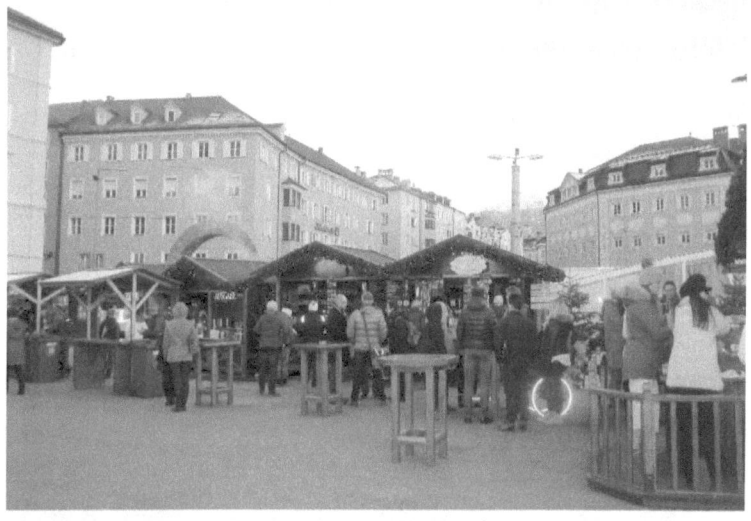

Dec 2018 Market square Christmas market Innsbruck ©Berna 2018

The *Christkindlmark*t – Christmas market – in Innsbruck is held from 15 Nov to 6 January, the day of the Three Holy Kings in the tradition visited the infant Jesus in the stable in Bethlehem.

The main Christmas market in Innsbruck is in the old market square.

Innsbruck was established as a market place in 1133 when the Counts of Andechs bought a field on the left bank of the Inn, today called St. Nikolaus.

In 1180 they swopped land with the Priory of Wilten to make a market on the Southern bank.

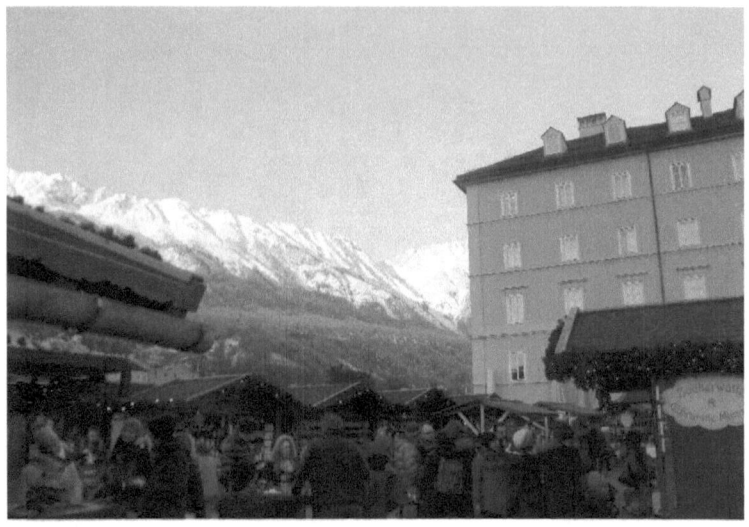

Dec 2018 Market square Christmas market, Innsbruck. The Nordkette mountain range with the ski pistes up behind.
©Berna 2018

The market and the trading rights were mentioned in a document in 1187 and between this year and 1205 the market eventually got city rights. Innsbruck became a privileged town, not just a field with trading rights.

With the important trans Alpine trading over the Brenner Pass there would also have been a December market, but whether you would characterize this as a "Christmas market" with the same festivities as in nearby Munich we do not know. But it is more than likely they had a Christmas market in their own way.

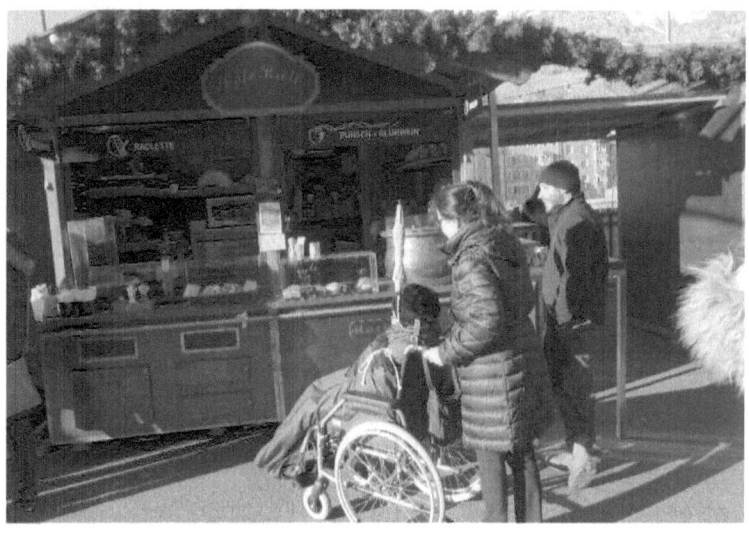

Dec 2018 Rediscovering the childhood Christkindl Markt Innsbruck ©Berna 2018

The Christmas market is a very popular activity here in Innsbruck and attracts all kinds of people.

The disabled are thoroughly packed in blankets to allow them to be wheeled around to relive thee wonders of their youth.

The attendant is also well coated in a thick padded coat, because the wheeling is not continuous exercise.

Luckily there is good cakes and roasted almonds at hand.

In the Christmas market on the market square is a Swarovski Christmas tree with 100.000 lights.

The Swarovski head office is just North of Innsbruck, in Wattens. Swarovski is a world wide high end chain marketing crystals, jewelry, watches, home accessories and - yes, Christmas ornaments.

You can't come closer to Christmas than here in Innsbruck!

There is a Swarovski Crystal World exhibition over in the old town as well as Swarovski store.

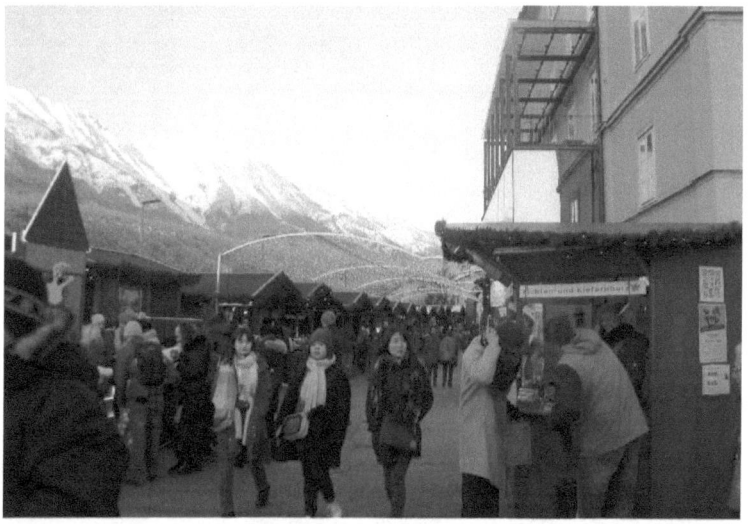

Dec 2018 Market square Christmas market, Innsbruck.
Nordkette mountain range with the skiing pists up behind.
©Berna 2018

Up behind the Christmas market and Innsbruck you see the *Nordkette* – the Alpine mountain range famous for its ski resorts.

It was up here the Winter Olympics were held in 1964 and again in 1976. The city is in 574m altitude and there is a lovely mountain air.

It forms an incredible frame or back curtain for the Christmas market and the town. Even here in Winter there are many tourists that have come from afar to enjoy the scenery.

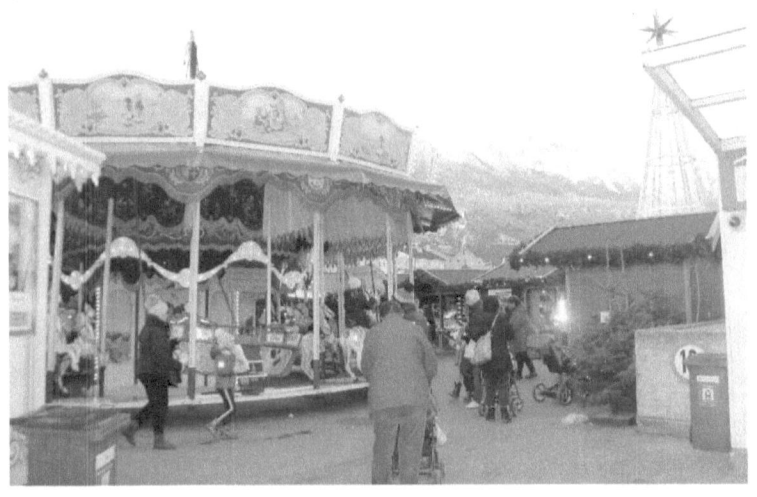

Dec 2018 Market square Christmas market, Innsbruck ©Berna 2018

There are of course the traditional amusements for the children, like a carrousel.

Other entertainments is a puppet theater, in German of course, which the children absolutely loved.

Austrian children are generally outgoing and friendly up here. There is a very cosmopolitan and friendly atmosphere no doubt because of the many tourists.

Modern Austria is much smaller than when it was an empire. The Second Republic was established in 1955.

But the Austrians are some of the most polite and friendly people in all Europe and have a modern welfare state.

The Tyrolians in Southern Austria have always had a special status. They are a happy and jolly lot, known all over the world for their special singing traditions and the *jodeln* - a singing without text.

The emperor was very fond of these peasants and granted them special rights – they were free of military duty for the empire and only had to serve to protect their own lands, Tyrol.

Christkindlmarkt am Altstadt

We use again the Austrian words *Christkindlmarkt am Altstadt* for the Christmas Child market in the Old Town of Innsbruck.

There are usually at least four Christmas markets in Innsbruck, and the next one is in the old town – the Altstadt, just as you cross from the bridge.

The Altstadt – the Old Town – is rich in what is called imperial architecture – buildings from the period Innsbruck was the favored town of the Habsburg emperors of the Holy Roman Empire.

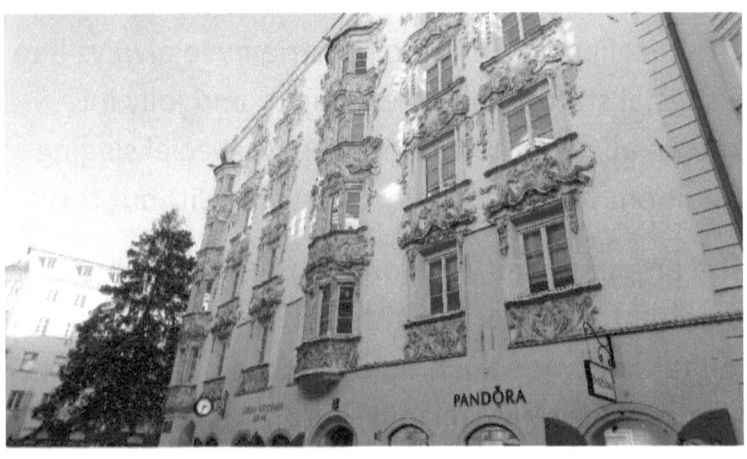

Imperial building style on the Herzog-Friedrich-Strasse in the Old Town, Innsbruck ©Berna 2018

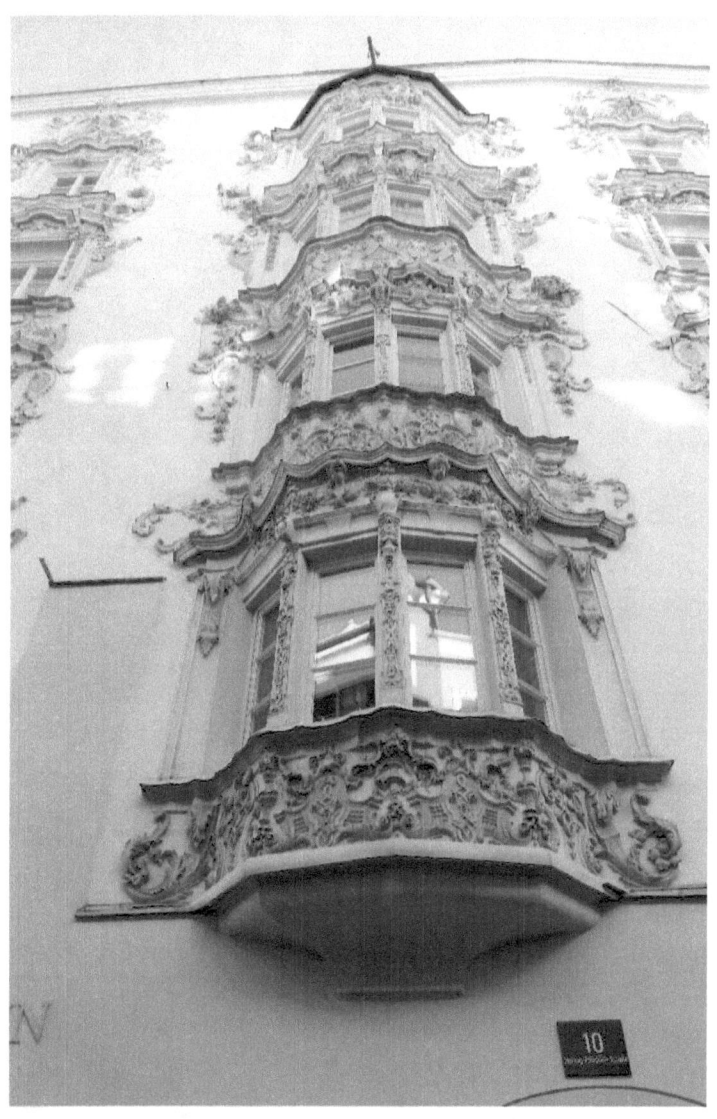

Bay window, detail from previous picture. ©Berna 2018

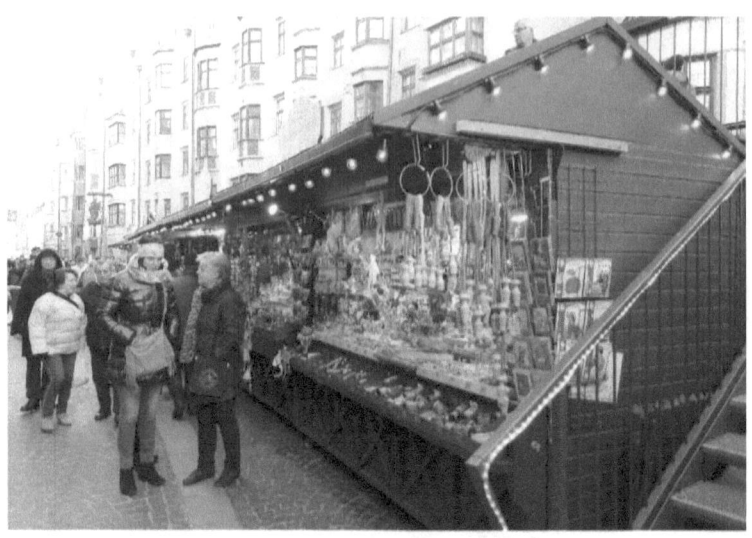

Dec 2018 Christkindl Markt im Altstadt – Christmas market in the Old Town, Innsbruck ©Berna 2018

The grand buildings in Herzog-Friedrich-Strasse flank the large traditional Christmas market in the Old Town – Altstadt – of Innsbruck.

Herzog-Friedrich-Strasse later becomes Maria-Theresien-Strasse, which is defined as having its own separate more futuristic Christmas market.

Maria-Theresien-Strasse is especially known for its large variety of fashion shops, with outlets for all the greatest brands in the World. It is true to the tradition of Innsbruck as the most important trading post in the posh Tyrol ski center.

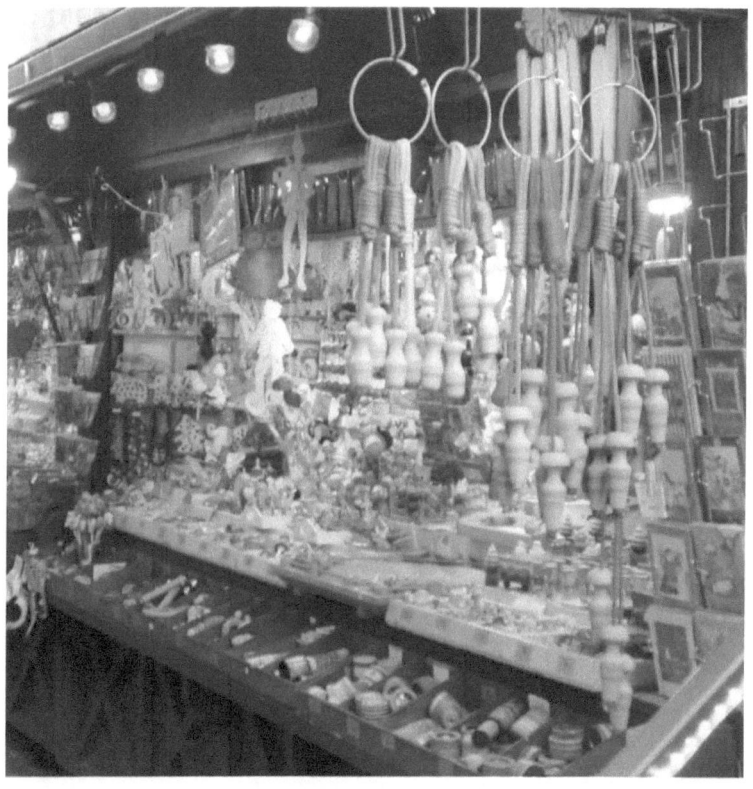

Dec 2018 Stall in the Christkindl Markt – Christmas market in Altstadt Innsbruck ©Berna 2018

There are over 70 stalls here, with all kinds of offers - food and drink, and of course ornaments of all kinds.

There are already so many shops with everything you could possibly want, and then you enter this Medieval tradition that founded Innsbruck back in 1133.

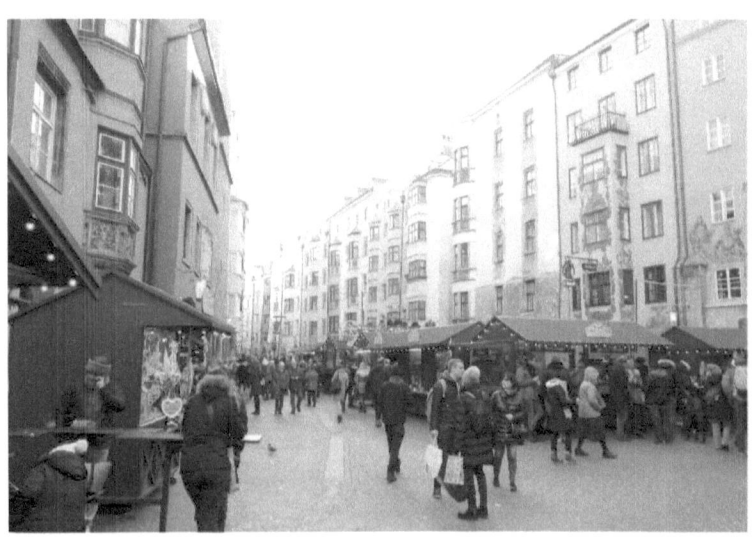

Dec 2018 Christkindl Markt – Christmas market in the Old Town, Innsbruck ©Berna 2018

The Christmas market has things of course that you don't usually find in the shops, but it is the experience, and joyous mood and laughter, the Austrian brass bands and the singing that makes the Christmas market into such a great experience. The tourists enjoy to come and participate in the local festivity and are welcomed by the locals.

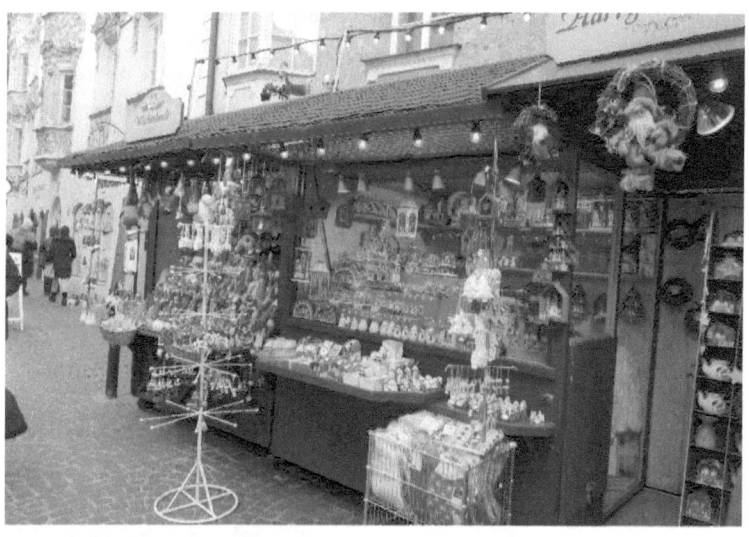

Dec 2018 Christkindl Markt - Christmas market in the Old Town, Innsbruck ©Berna 2018

Here is a traditional stall with Christmas ornaments.

The ornaments are not all traditional, but in great variety, humorous and happy.

There are key rings, small Santa figurines, angels, snow men, polar bears, you name it, they have it.

There are also traditional carved wooden figurines, the Tyrolian specialty that is proudly exported to many other Christmas markets, see *Christmas Nativities Luxembourg and Trier.*

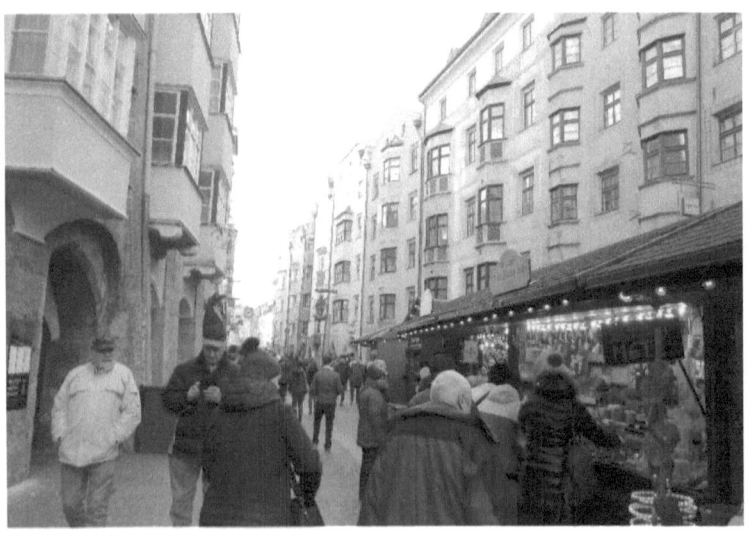

Dec 2018 Christkindl Markt – Christmas market in Herzog-Friedrich-Strasse in the Old Town, Innsbruck

Locals and tourists meet and mix here. You here languages from all over the World.

Everybody comes, more than a million each year, to visit the Christmas markets in Innsbruck.

Some are regulars that also come here for the great skiing or even have their own chalet or Winter holiday apartment.

They appreciate the peace and security and the friendliness.

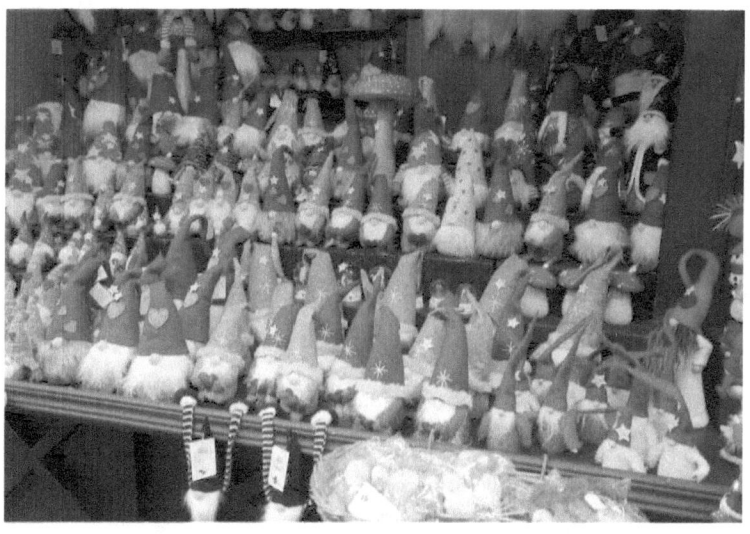

Dec 2018 stall at the Christkindl Markt, Old Town, Innsbruck
©Berna 2018

Here a detail from a stall selling Santa figurines.

The variety is impressive. Although the theme is a friendly Santa with a long, pointed hat with stars, the variation over the theme is truly artistic.

You are sure to find one that suits just your taste and is not just like all the others.

And so it is from stall to stall. They overflow with exiting offers that make the Christmas market a special occasion.

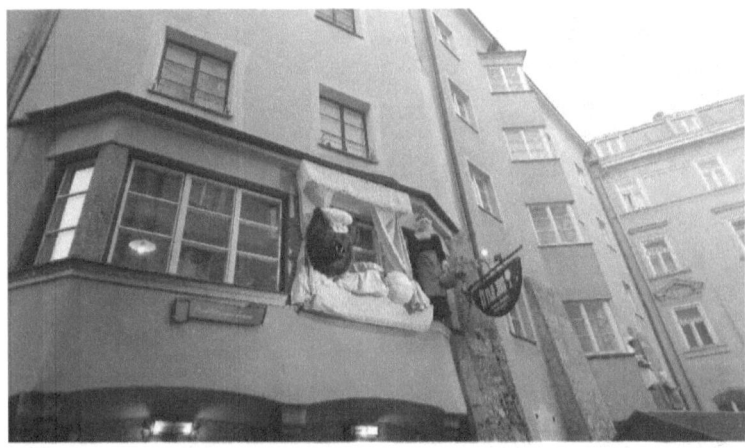

Dec 2018 Christkindl Markt – Christmas market decoration, Old Town, Innsbruck ©Berna 2018

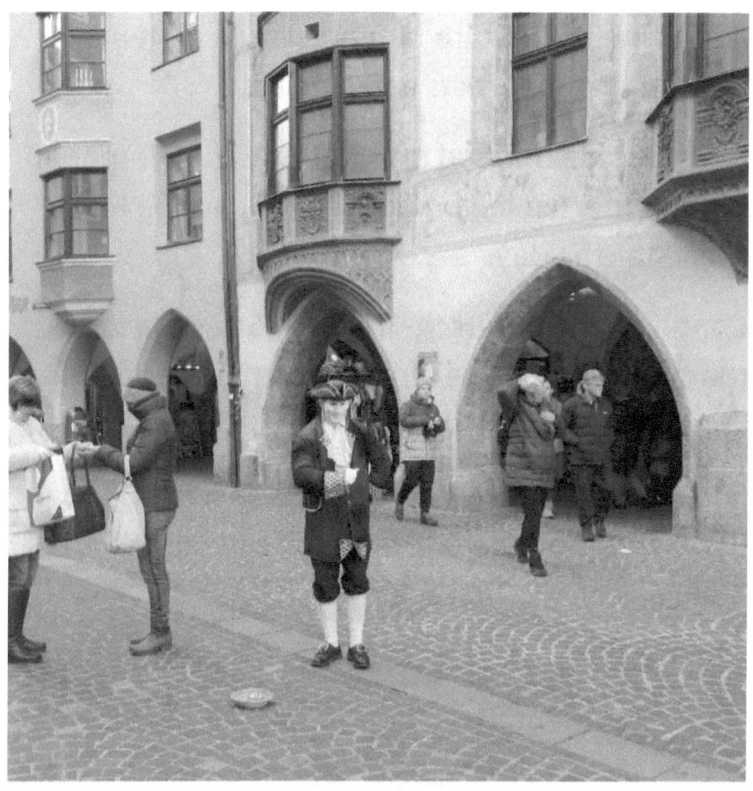

Dec 2018 Street entertainer Herzog-Friedrich-Strasse, Innsbruck ©Berna 2018

Up there are surprising and amusing decorations in a theme that surely must have been agreed by the many merchants in this town.

It is worth coming here just for the inspiration.

As has been a feature of markets since Medieval times there are artists and jugglers.

Here a Roma dressed in a costume from Imperial times, entertaining onlookers and earning his bread for the day.

Continue down Herzog-Friedrich-Strass, cross Martgraben and the street becomes Marie-Theresien-Strass with all the fancy shops.

For the discerning visitor there is special window decorations on the buildings, placed outside the buildings on the first floor.

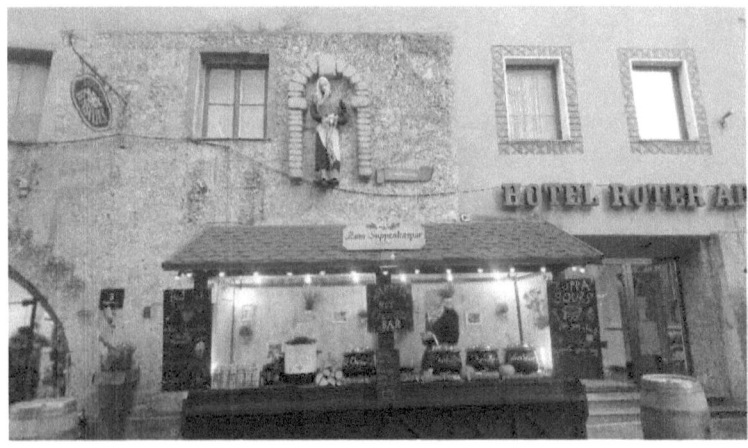

Hotel Roter Adler, Seilergasse 6, Innsbruck ©Berna 2018

At first you are surprised, and then thrilled, and you have to remember to look up also, not just look straight ahead at the stalls and shop windows.

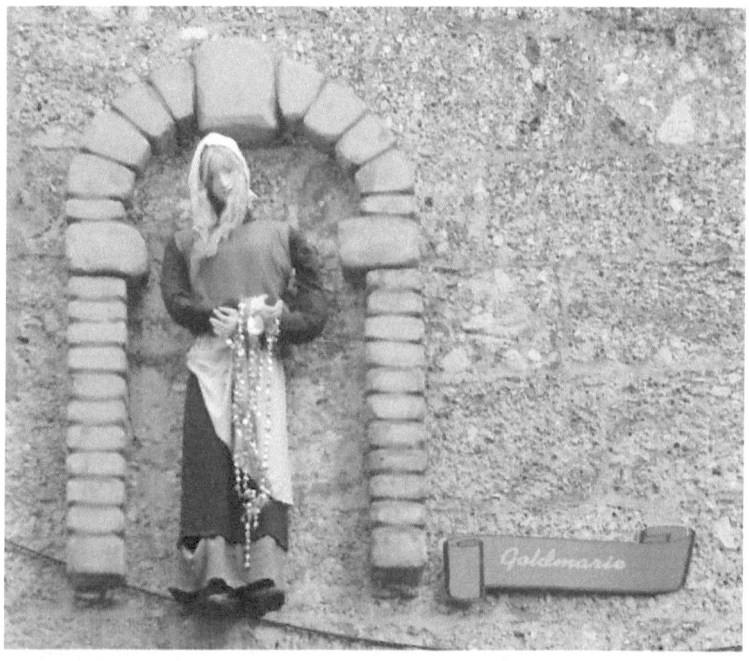

Goldmaria, Hotel Roter Adler, Seilergasse 6, Innsbruck ©Berna 2018

On the wall by the Hotel Roter Adler, one of the more than 70 hotels in Innsbruck, is a surprising figurine, again on the first floor height, over the restaurant, wonderfully lit and cozy looking.

It is a demurely looking blond girl in traditional long skirted costume, carrying a large rosary with crystals.

The artistic level and quality in Innsbruck will meet all discerning taste, as the reader can see in the book *Christmas Nativities Innsbruck*.

Without being snobbish the Tyrolians love for art and handicrafts that has been passed down many generations.

You see it in the buildings, in the shops, in the Christmas market – it retains its imperial heritage.

Some cities and countries you visit that have been former empires feel like they are missing something, and many of their people feel inferior because of the loss.

But not the Tyrolians!

They proudly display what they have but remember they were themselves before the empire. Innsbruckers were busy traders long before the empire and continue their traditions.

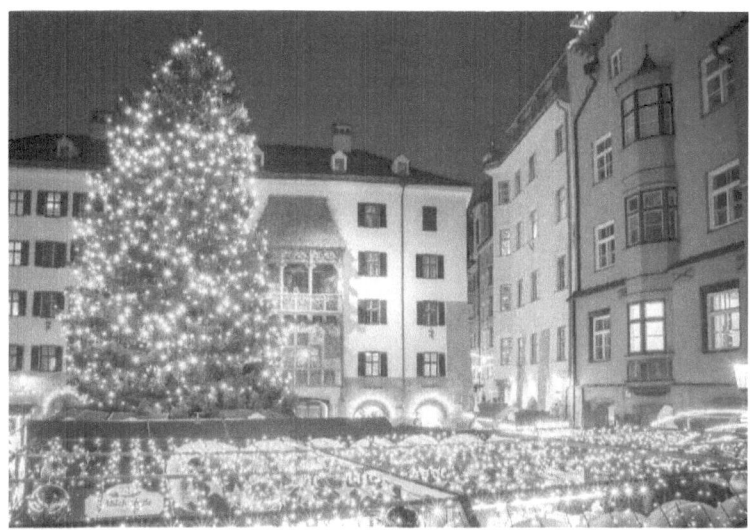

The Christmas season in Innsbruck's old town is traditional, romantic and atmospheric. Directly in front of the *Goldener Dachl* - Golden Roof, the Christmas market stalls are nestled against the medieval houses.

The stalls are a treasure trove of Christmas tree decorations, handicrafts, woolen goods and souvenirs. A viewing platform offers a wonderful view over the roofs of the huts. Tower musicians conjure up atmospheric moments from the Golden Roof with traditional Christmas music.

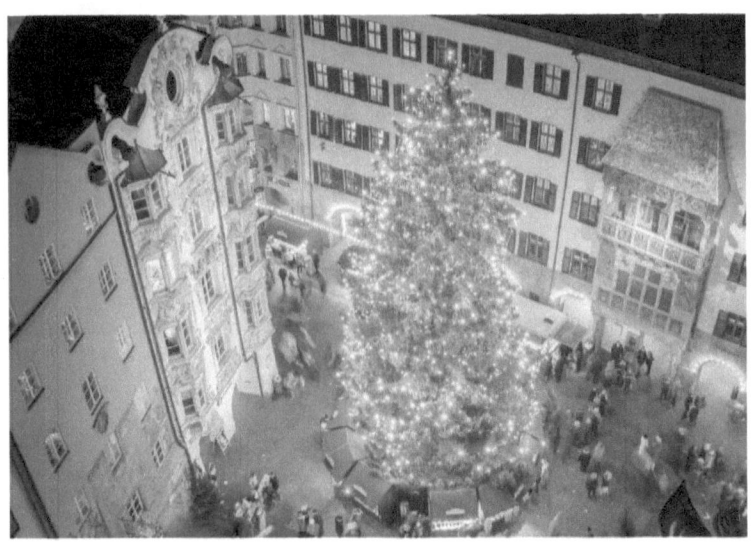

a beautiful view don to the Goldener Dachl and the Christmas tree.

A modern sea of lights welcomes Christmas market visitors to Maria-Theresien-Strasse. Numerous trees are covered in small lights and line Maria-Theresien-Strasse. A wide variety of market stalls provide visitors with international gift ideas. Anyone looking for a special souvenir is sure to find one here. The aromas of mulled wine and the hearty snacks also compete to be best..

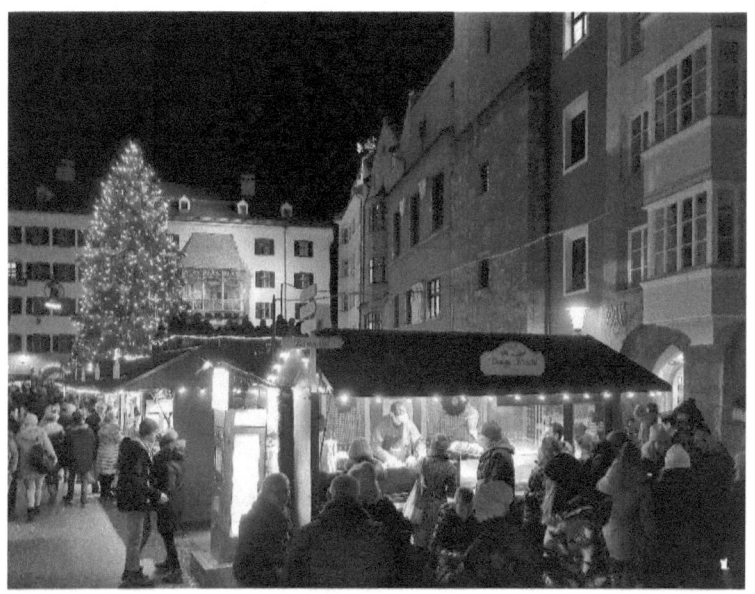

The medieval houses of Innsbruck's Old Town Christkindlmarkt provide the framework for what is probably the most traditional Christmas market in the city. 64 Christmas stalls form lines beneath the light-festooned Christmas tree.

This Christmas market is also perfectly located for your Christmas shopping. If you are on a shopping spree and wandering through the shops on Maria-Theresien-Straße, this is the ideal place to take a break.

43

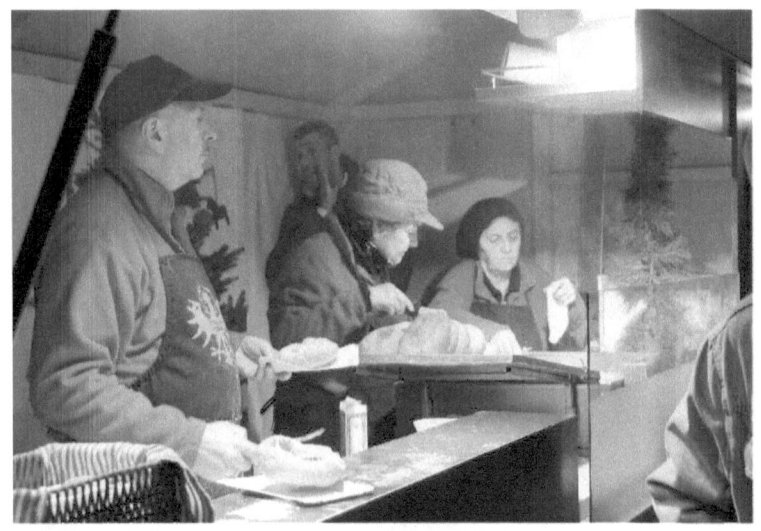

For a Christmas market with kids, the thrilling attractions and cosy atmosphere of the Christkindlmarkt make it an experience for the whole family.

The visitors can discover alternative craftsmanship, Xmas products and down-to-earth culinary fayre.

With the trumpets sounding from the Goldener Dachl - Golden Roof, the sense of ancient homeland can be felt all around while you grab a local Bretzel snack.

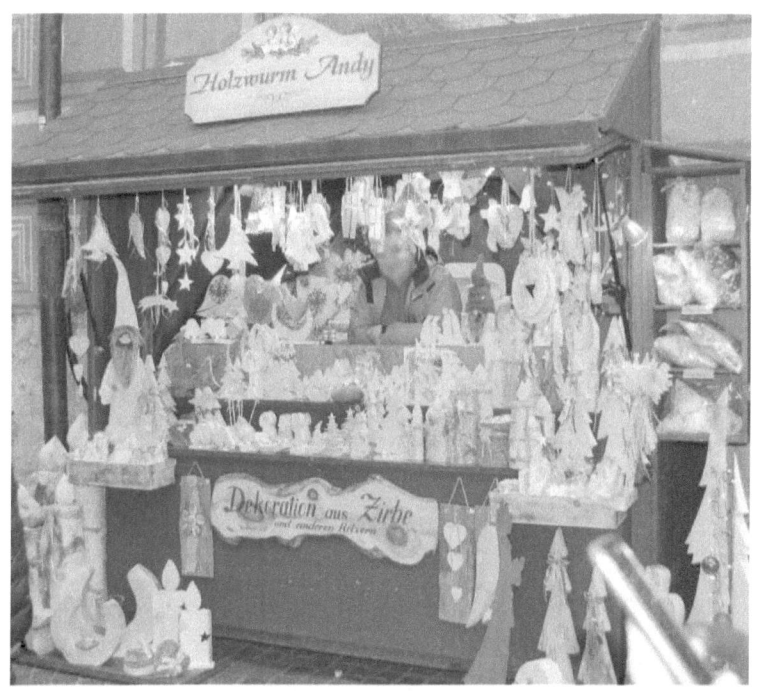

Scented almonds, lovingly carved nativity figures and colourful felt hats: the Christmas Market is all about folk art

Everywhere you turn in Innsbruck you are met by the Christmas Angels. The young people in golden angel costumes spread this special Christmas spirit and a very special festive splendour.

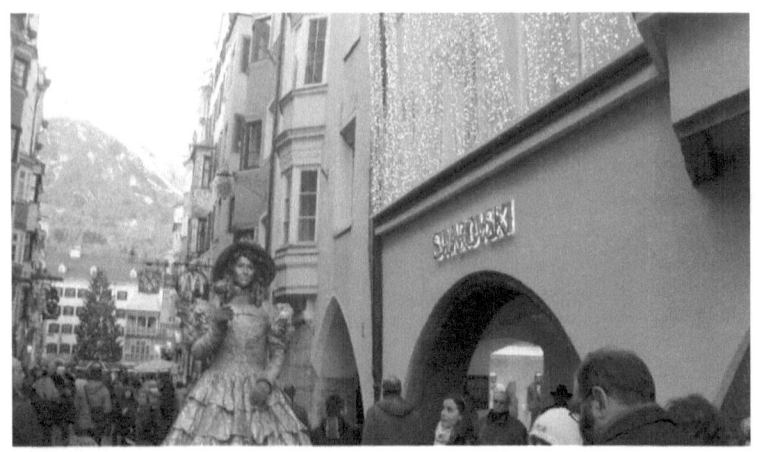

A live statue with the Goldener Dachl – Golden Roof in the background.

To the right thee Swarovski store.

This global business is said to employ 5,000 people here in Innsbruck alone.

Recall the old folk tale story of the Seven Dwarves that went to their gem mine every morning and toiled until nightfall, excavating the most beautiful and precious stones you could imagine.

And how they locked them up carefully and hung the key on a nail next to the door!

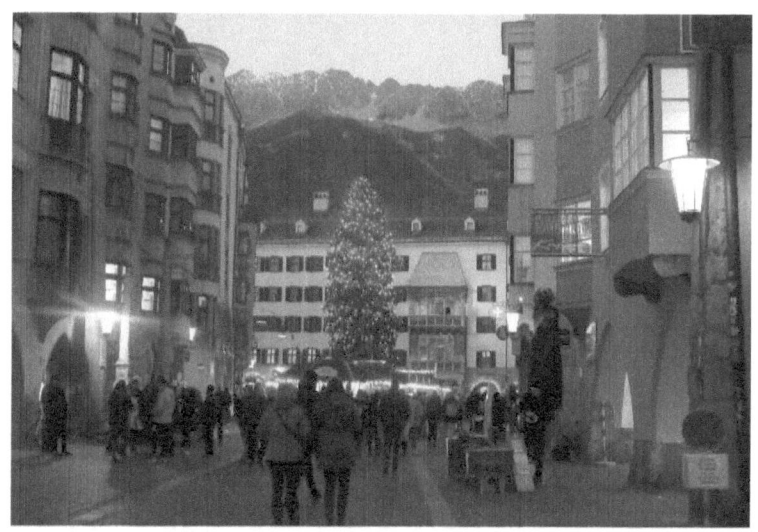

You can hear Christmas Music:

Daily at 5.30 p.m.

Traditional brass music from the Golden Roof

Daily at 6 p.m.

Performance by the Innsbruck Music School on the Fairy Tale Stage

Getting cold

It is winter and the cool and fresh mountain air may chill you a bit, but there is a great solution to everything, you will see!

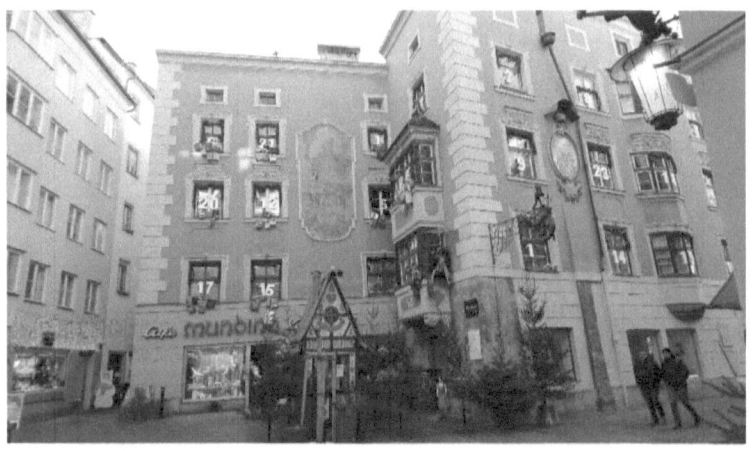

Dec 2018 "Calendar House", Kiebachgasse 16, Innsbruck
©Berna 2018

This wonderful old house in Kiebachgasse 16, in Mundingplatzl in the *Altstadt*, is decorated as a Christmas calendar.

Each window has a number, just like the carton Christmas calendars you get with your newspaper for your kids.

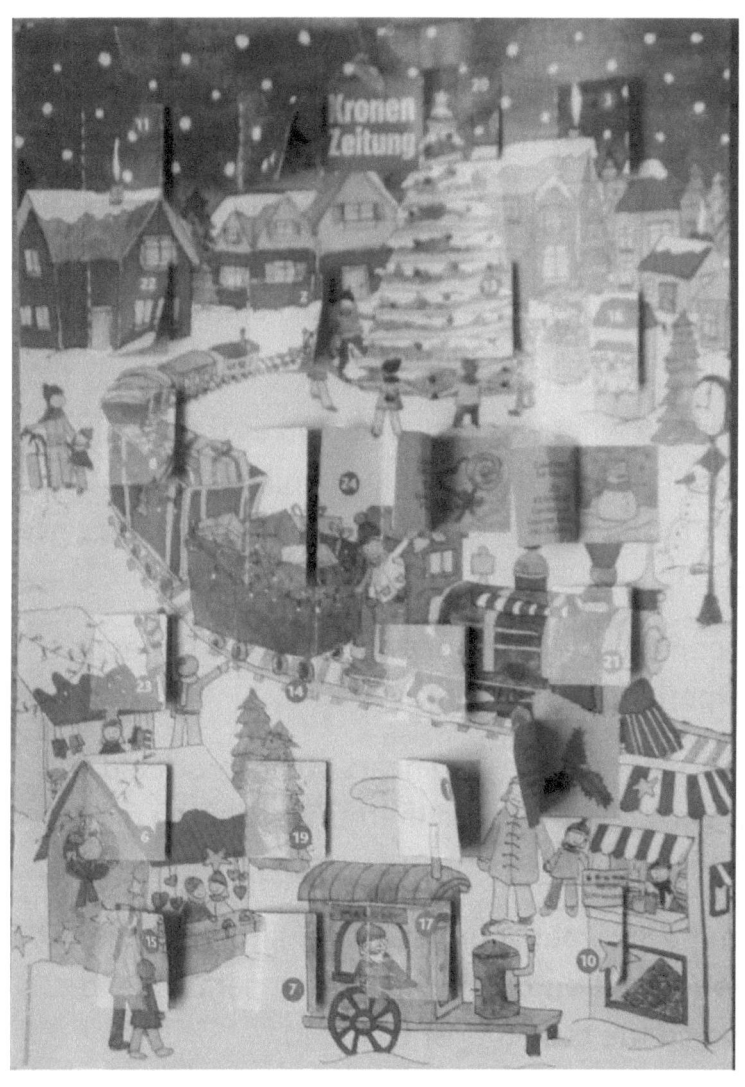

Christmas calendar for the children, from the newspaper
Austrian *Kronen Zeitung* 2018

By each window is a different Christmas decoration. Although all the windows are open, you still enjoy the different surprises.

In this building is also Munding, the oldest café in Tyrol. It was established in when Napoleon was ravaging Europe and France sold Louisiana to the United States, doubling its territory.

Here, in what was earlier known as the GUMPPHAUS, the Munding family has carried on the business of Tirol's oldest Konditorei-Café since 1803.

Open the window – or door! – to this fantastic experience!

The café is in the very heart of Innsbruck old town, only a hundred metres west of the famous Golden Roof.

In the Summer your needs are different and then you can sit outdoors under great parasols and watch the busy tourist traffic.

There are many other good cafés in this area, but Munding is especially famous, and for very good reason!

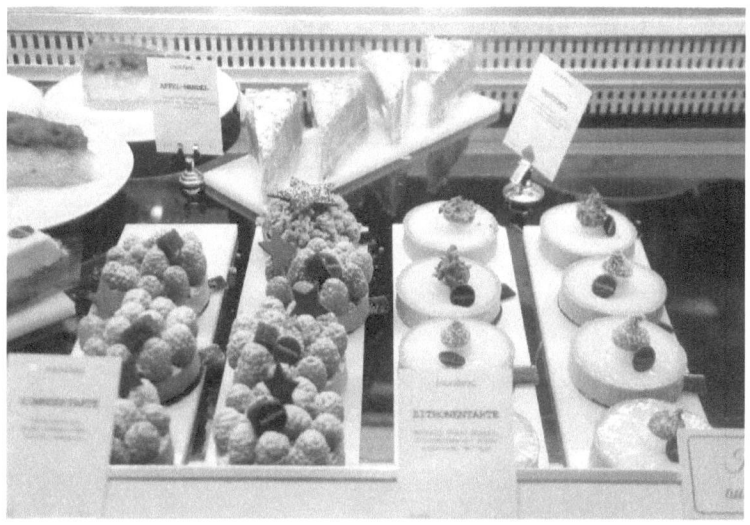

Dec 2018 Tartalets in Konditorei Munding, Innsbruck ©Berna 2018

Munding has a take away pastry shop – *konditorei* in Austrian - with the cake counter just by the entrance.

Here you find – as you do in many places in Austria, the most exquisite cakes.

To the left flashing red raspberry tartalets and to the right heavenly lemon tartalets.

Your eyes immediately make your mouth water! Luckily the outdoors will take care of some cake!

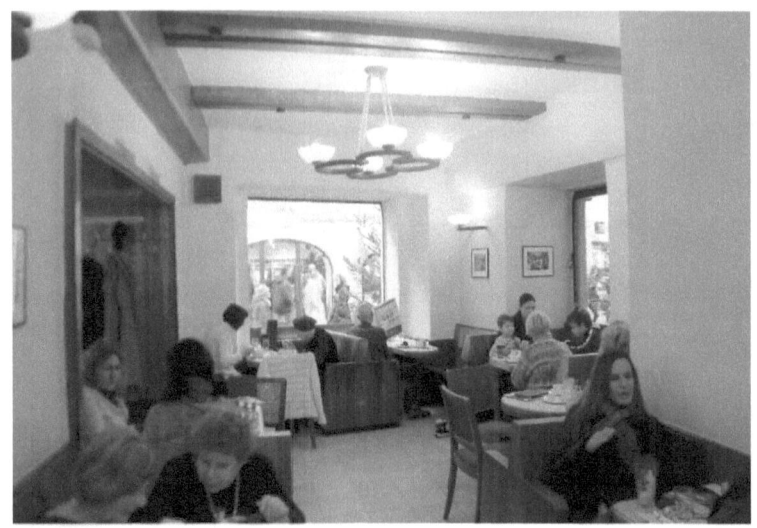

Dec 2018 Konditorei Munding, Innsbruck ©Berna 2018

Café Munding has a wonderful atmosphere. Here the locals mix with travelers from all over the world to relax and gossip and get warm again.

Café Munding has the best hot chocolate in the world, it is said. The world is a big place and you have to go through a lot of chocolate to make an informed judgment.

They bring scalding hot milk in a glass to your table and you add chocolate that has the consistency of a truffle to the milk.

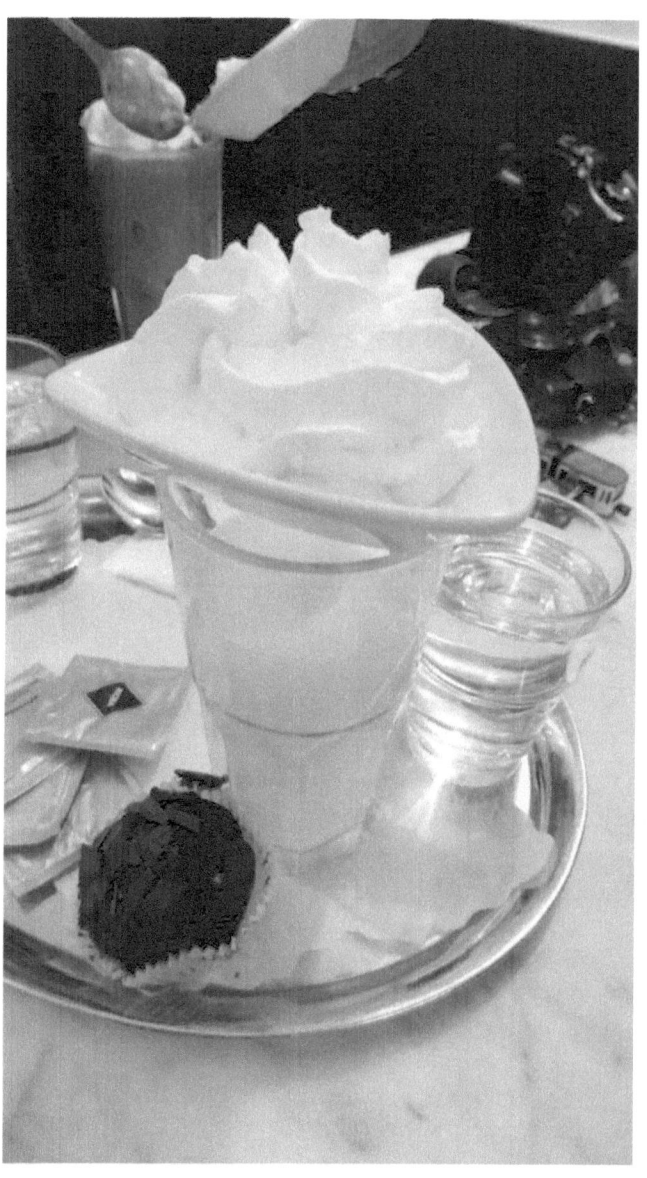

Dec 2018 Hot chocolate at Innsbruck Konditorei Munding
©Berna 2018

You then finish it off with a dollop of whipped cream.

To the left the truffle is being dissolved, whipped cream in the small assiette to the right the hot milk before the trick.

Beware children don't get scalded!

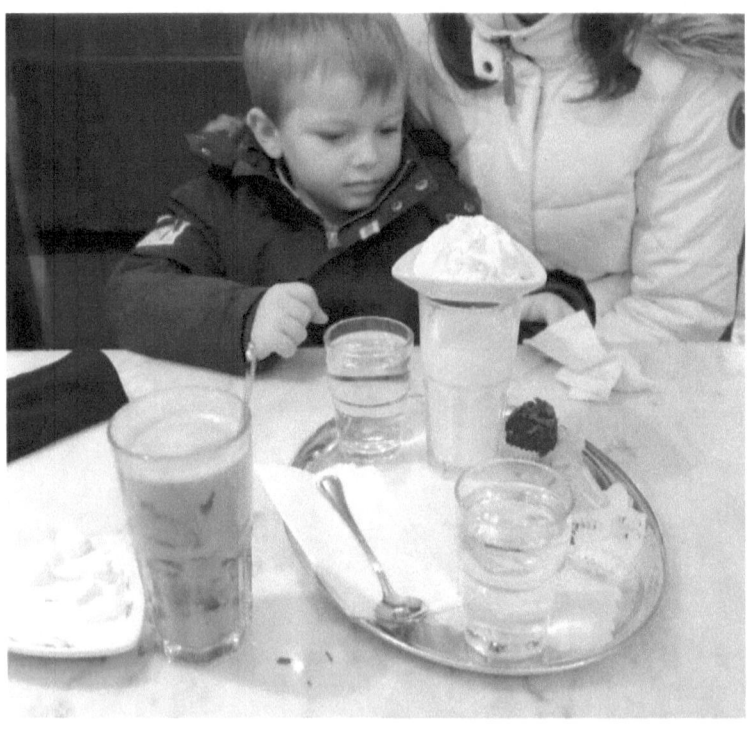

Watching the preparation of a hot chocolate at Munding.
©Berna 2018

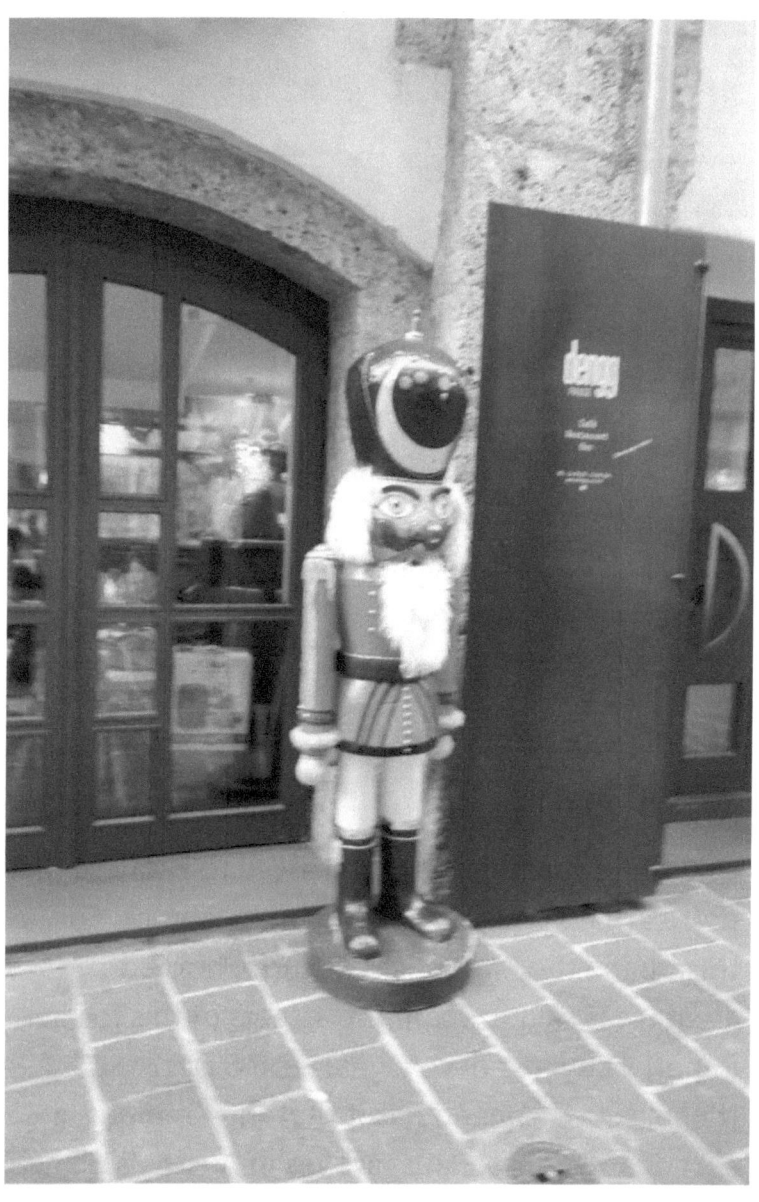

Dec 2018 "Animal" Santa Claus, Innsbruck ©Berna 2018

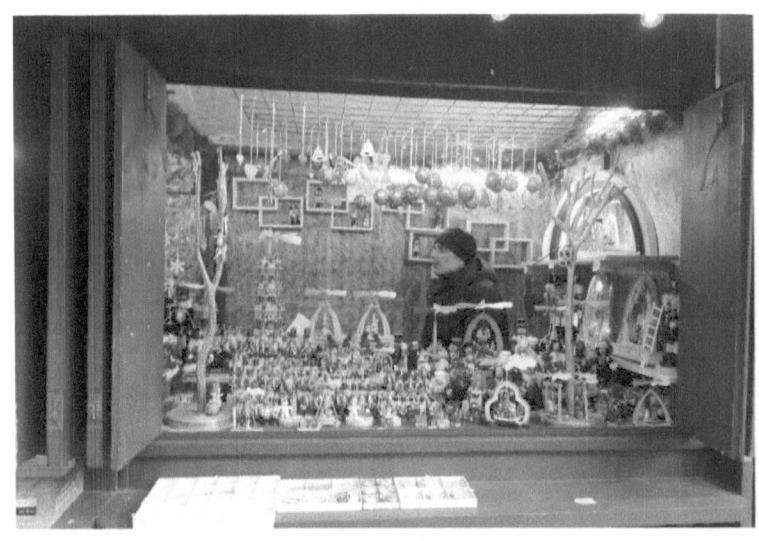

Traditional hand carved Christmas figurines in a shop window, Altstadt, Innsbruck ©Berna 2018

Duly refreshed you can now join the Christmas markets again.

One thing you might be interested to know, is that there are no naughty children in Innsbruck. For this, thank the Krampus. The furry, horned creature is said to roam the streets of this former imperial city just once a year—on 5 Dec.- St. Nicholas Eve. Legend has it that the Krampus, a sort of anti-Santa Claus, arrives in Austria's western Tyrol region with a sack of coal, in search of mischievous children.

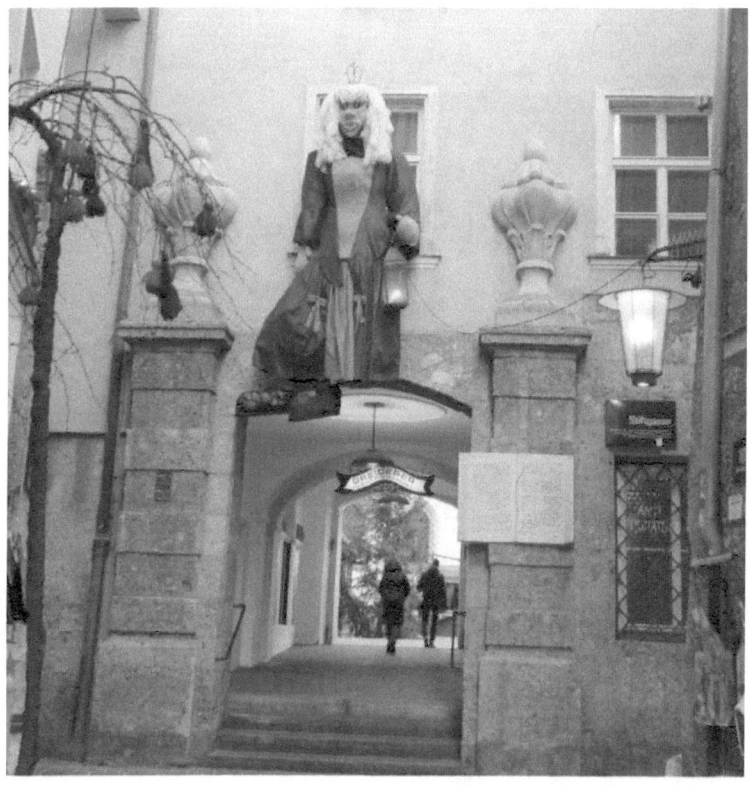

Dec 2018 Christmas decoration, Innsbruck Altstadt – the old town - ©Berna 2018

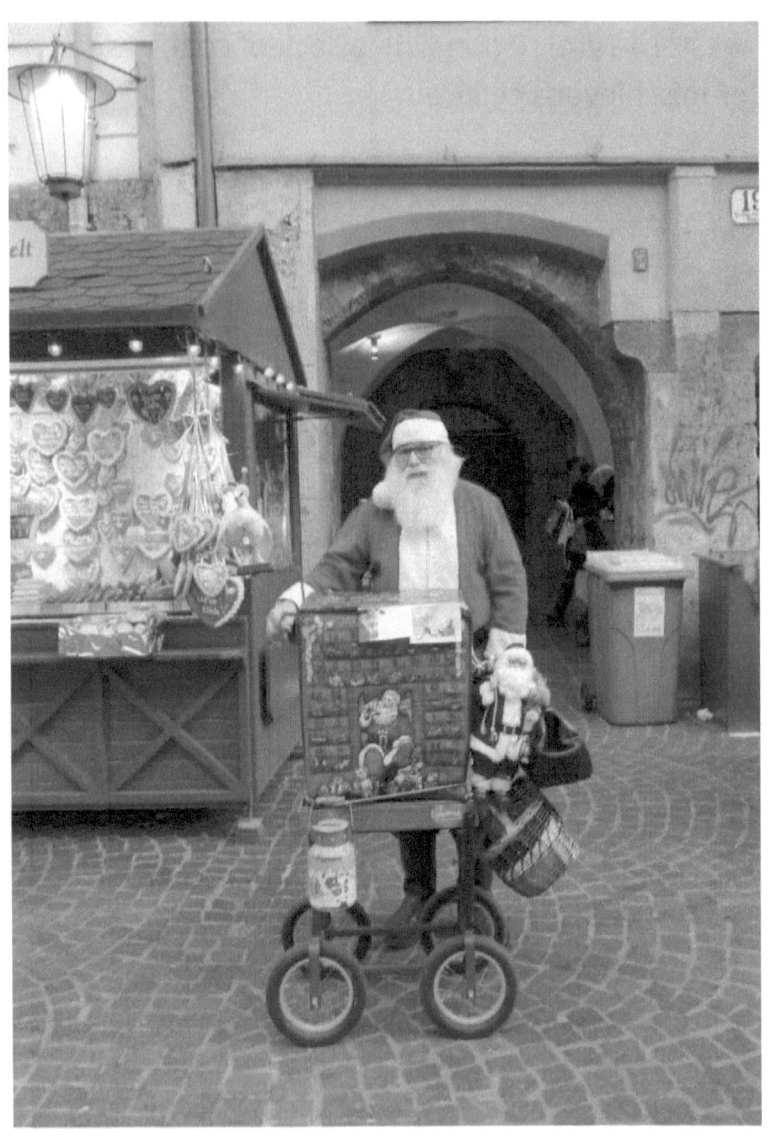

Dec 2018   Santa organ-grinder Innsbruck old town   ©Berna 2018

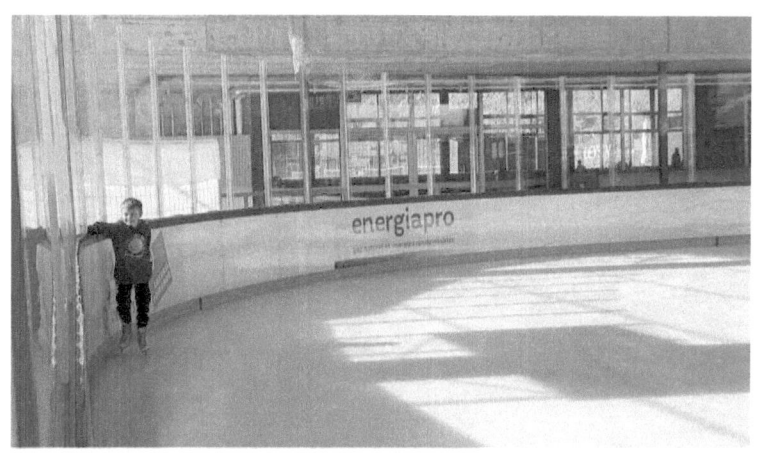

There is an Olympic skating rink in Innsbruck where you can hone your skating skills or just have fun.

Perhaps the reader is interested in our family book "Learn to Ski With Me"? See   ISBN 979-8-201-199-494 and in color print in the United States under ISBN 978-1-956-773-521.

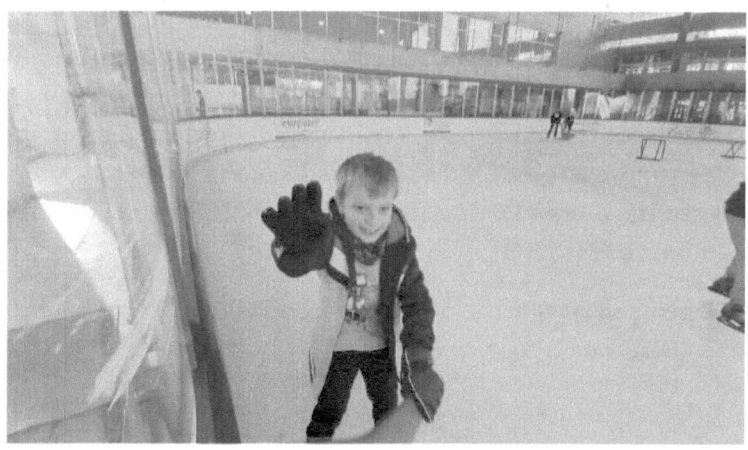

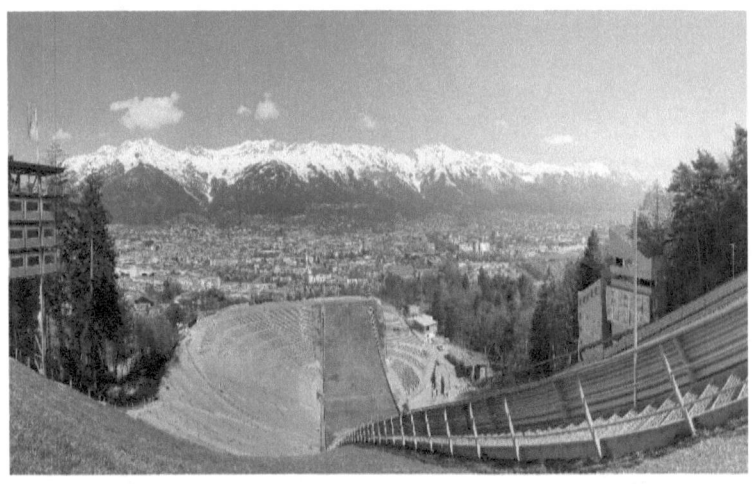

Innsbruck Panorama Nordkette from the signature ski jump that can be seen from all over Innsbruck.

Finds show that it was used early as a place of burnt offerings and as a settlement from the Neolithic period to the Iron Age.

In 1809, the Bergisel was the scene of the Battle of Bergisel four times under the command of the freedom fighter Andreas Hofer. In 1892, the Andreas Hofer Memorial was unveiled to commemorate these battles. The events of the third Battle of Bergisel on August 13, 1809 are depicted in the Innsbruck giant panorama.

According to legend, the battle between the two giants Haymon and Thyrsus took place here.

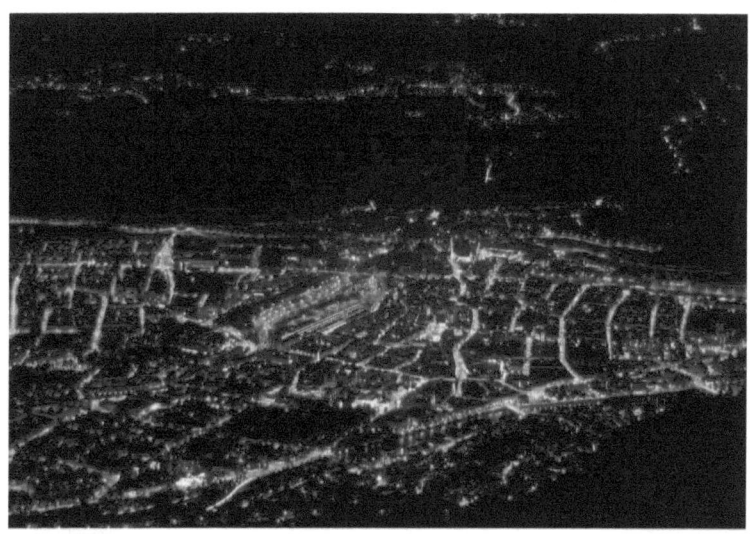

A panoramic view of Innsbruck from the same spot in the evening, with all the lights shining.

Innsbruck has been a venue for the Four Hills Tournament since 1952. After a smaller ski jump had already existed, the Bergisel ski jump was built from concrete for the 1964 Winter Olympics, which was also used for the 1976 Games. After this ski jump no longer met the requirements, a new ski jump was built according to plans by the architect Zaha Hadid and opened in 2002.

Until an accident following a mass panic in 1999, which initially claimed five lives and left another five young spectators in need of care, one of whom died four years later as a result of the accident, the Bergisel Stadium was also the venue for the snowboard spectacle Air & Style.

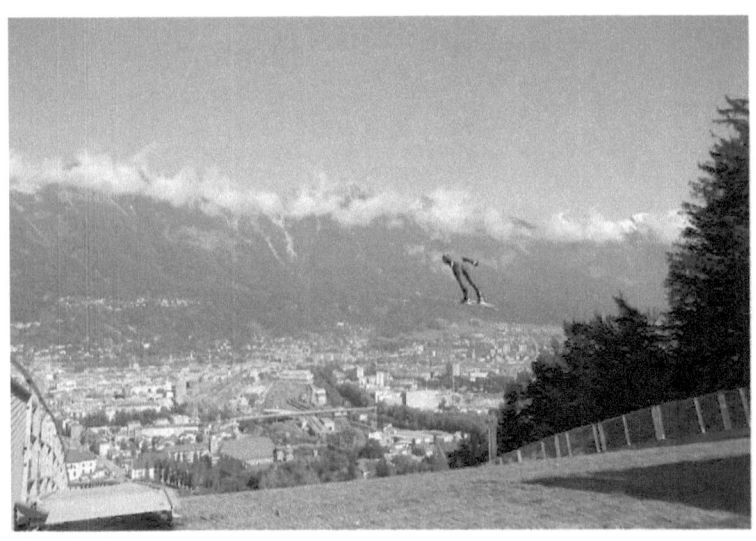

https://commons.wikimedia.org/wiki/File:Bergisel.jpg

Innsbruck has hosted major sporting events on several occasions. Tyrol is traditionally known for winter sports activities, and the Innsbruck Bergisel ski jump has been part of the annual Four Hills Tournament since 1952. With a few interruptions, Innsbruck has hosted one of the largest freestyle snowboard festivals in Europe, the Air & Style Contest, every year since 1994.

In 2005, the city hosted the international winter student games, the Winter Universiade. Also in 2005, Innsbruck hosted the men's ice hockey world championships together with Vienna.

The largest sporting competitions ever held in Innsbruck include the only two Winter Olympics ever held in Austria, in 1964 and 1976.

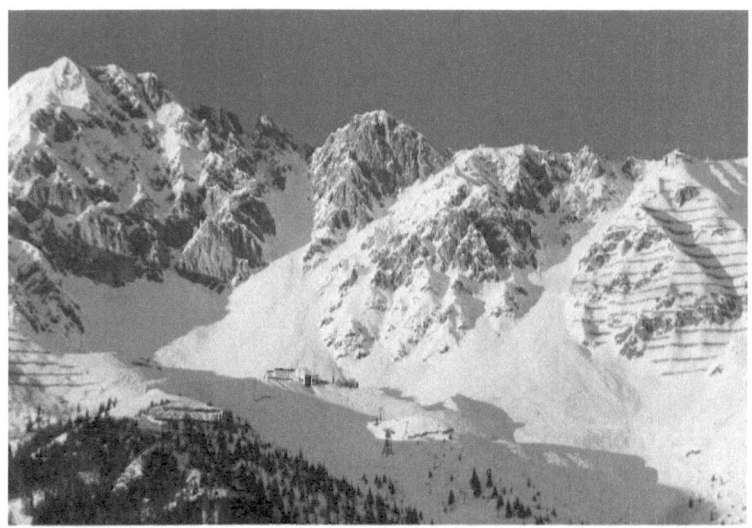

The Innsbruck Nordkette cable cars in Tyrol provide access to the Nordkette, the southernmost mountain range of the Karwendel.

They run in three sections from the city center of Innsbruck, via the Hungerburg district, to the Seegrube station (1905 m above sea level), and then on to the Hafelekar mountain station (2269 m above sea level). Section 1, from the old town of Innsbruck to the Hungerburg, is accessible via the "Hungerburgbahn" cable car, sections 2 and 3, to the Seegrube station and to the Hafelekar, via two cable cars with a total of three cabins.

The first preliminary concessions for the construction of a cable car from the Hungerburg to the Hafelekar were granted at the beginning of the 20th century. In 1925, Karl Innerebner discussed his project of a cable car to the Hafelekar.

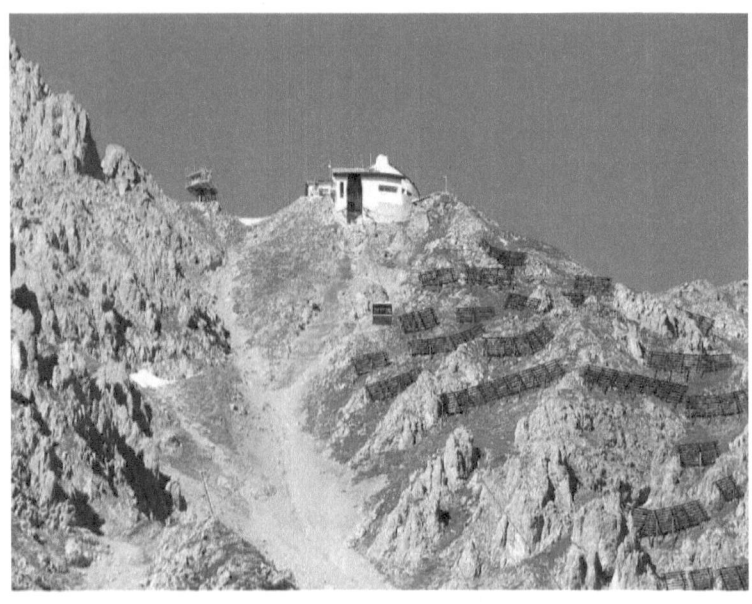

https://commons.wikimedia.org/wiki/File:Nordkettenbahn_Sektion2.jpg

The renovation of the facilities was announced as an international competition in 2004, which concluded in December of that year with the winning project being realized. The British-Iraqi architect Zaha Hadid, who also designed the new Bergisel ski jump in Innsbruck, took the lead in the architectural design. From the end of 2005, work on the slightly modified design was carried out as part of a public-private partnership. The Innsbrucker Nordkettenbahnen GmbH, a subsidiary of the city of Innsbruck, STRABAG and Leitner AG were involved. STRABAG will operate the cable car for a limited period of time, after which the facilities will revert to the city of Innsbruck. The work was completed with the commissioning of the new facilities in December 2006.

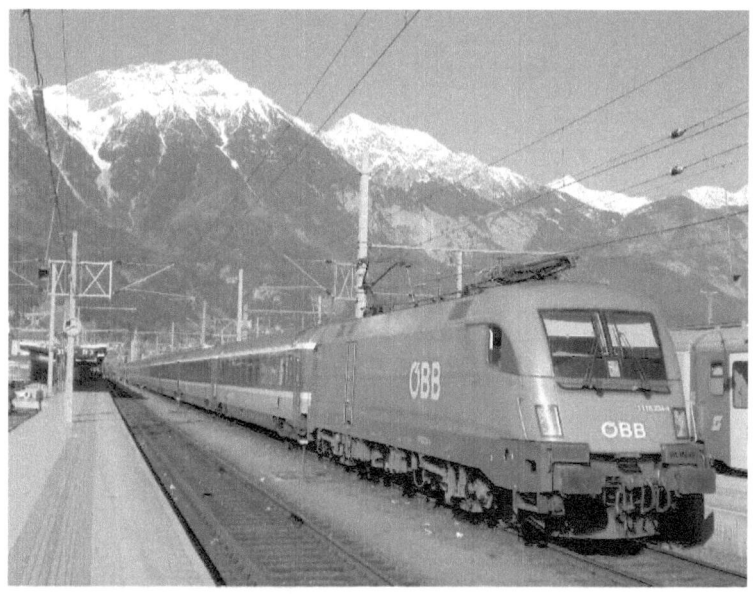

Foor train lovers and train spotters there is a lot of interesting activity at the Innsbruck Central Station – Innsbruck Hauptbahnhof.

This train is the ÖBB 1116 234-4 with SBB EC coaches as ÖBB EC 162 Transalpin on its way to Basel SBB, in Innsbruck Hbf (main station).

With the opening of the Lower Inn Valley Railway via Kufstein to Munich and Salzburg in 1858, the city was connected to the rapidly developing railway network.

For the young you can buy wooden OBB trains in well assorted toy shops.

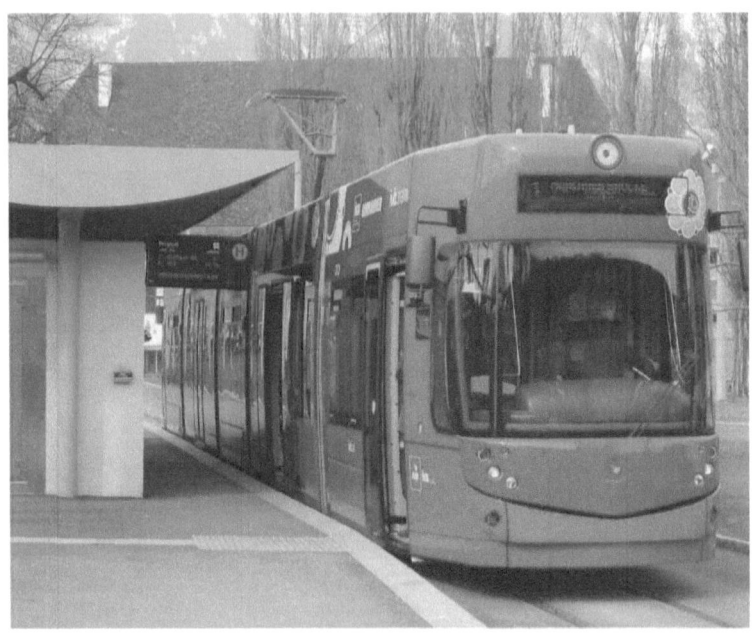

IVB tram car #351 of type 'Bombardier Flexity Outlook Innsbruck' as line 1 at Bergisel terminus.

In the city and its suburbs, tram and bus lines are operated by the Innsbruck Transport Company (IVB), Innbus, ÖBB-Postbus and other transport companies in the VVT transport association. After the regular lines have closed, there is a night bus network, the most important of which run all night long on all weekdays.

Silent Night

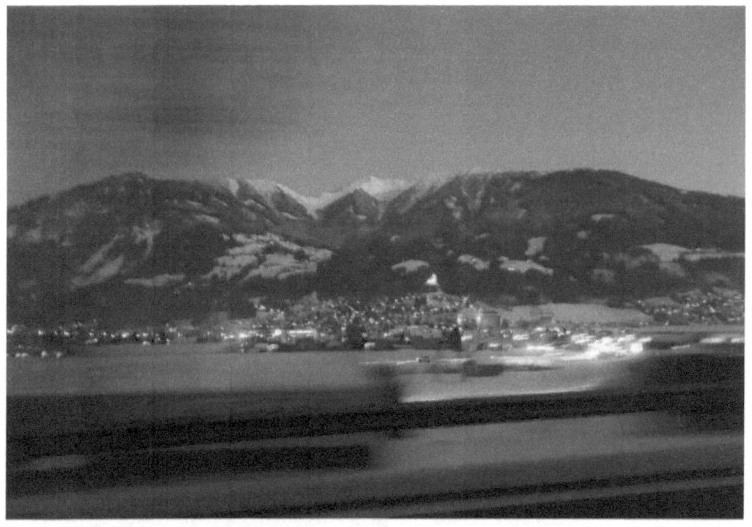

Dec 2018 Driving out of Innsbruck to the North ©Berna 2018

"Silent Night" – in German *Stille Nacht* - is a very popular Christmas carol, composed in 1818 by Franz Xaver Gruber to lyrics by Joseph Mohr in the small town of Oberndorf bei Salzburg.

It was declared an intangible cultural heritage by UNESCO in 2011.

Salzburg will be our next stop.

Christmas Market

Malaga

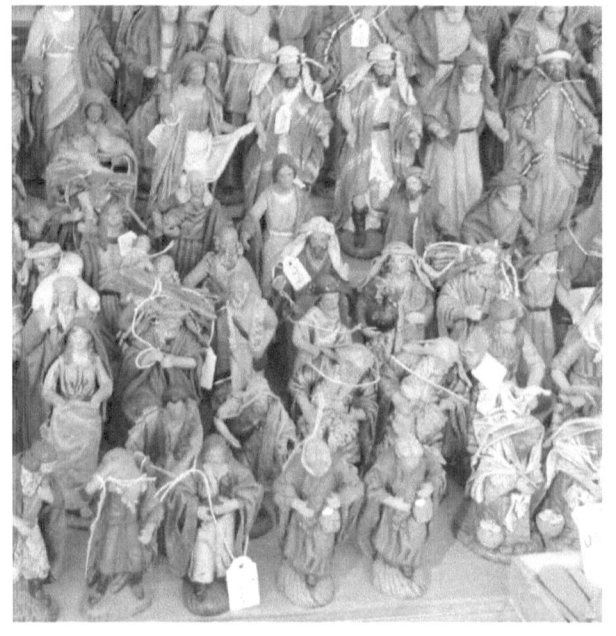

ISBN 978-5-1068-3525-1

Cristina Berna and Eric Thomsen

2024

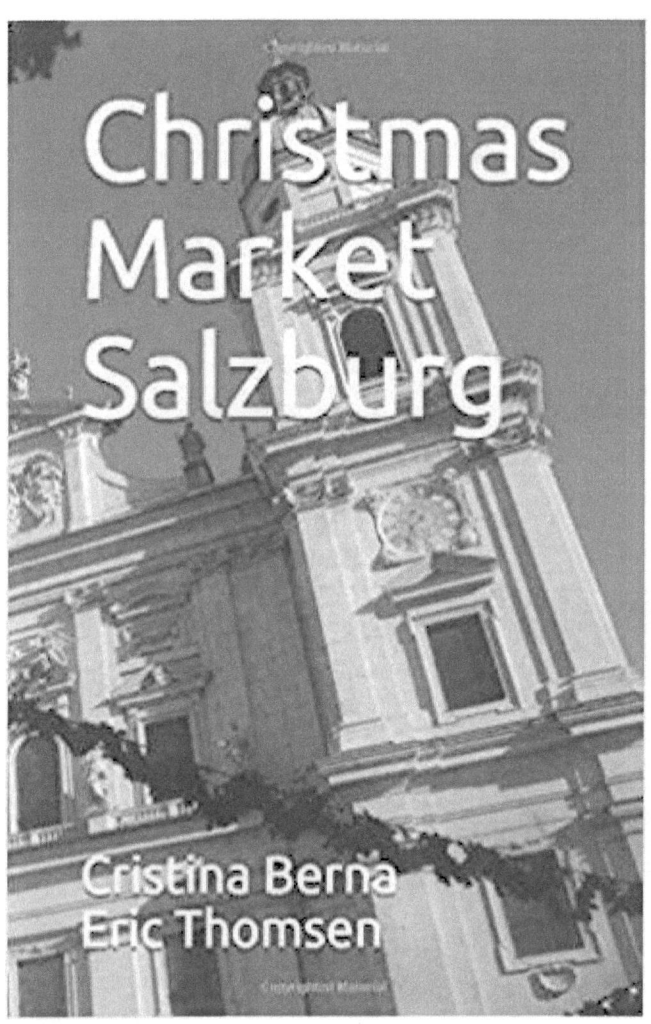

Christmas
Market
Salzburg

Cristina Berna
Eric Thomsen

ISBN

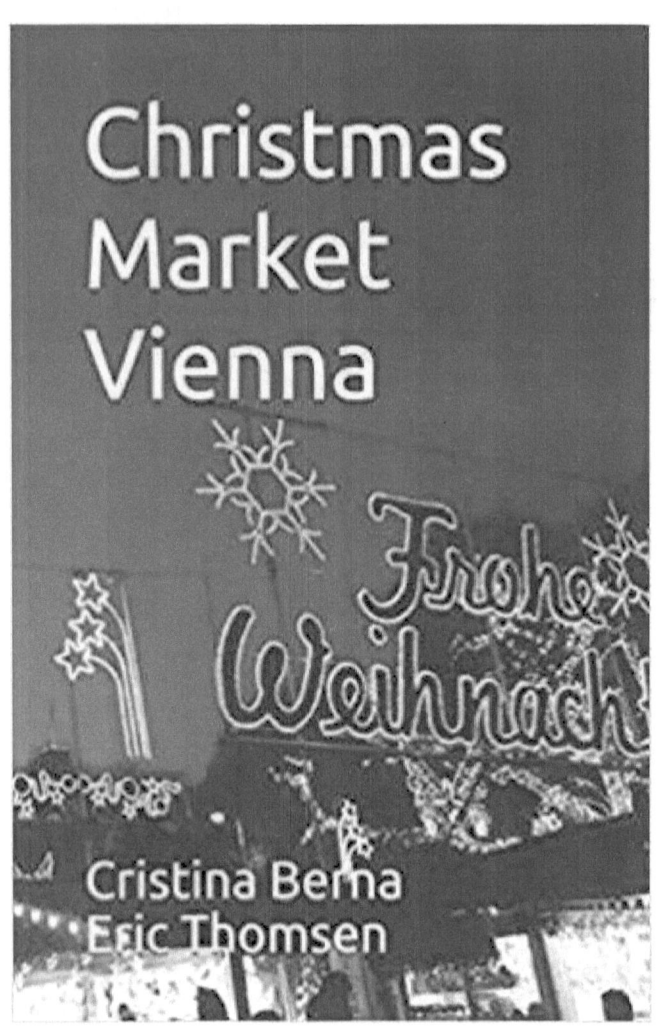

Christmas Market Vienna

Cristina Berna
Eric Thomsen

ISBN 978-1-386-103-196

www.ingramcontent.com/pod-product-compliance
Lightning Source LLC
Chambersburg PA
CBHW021020180526
45163CB00005B/2038